Group's

BODY-BUILDING

GUIDE TO

COMMUNITY

strengthening relationships in your church

Loveland, Colorado
www.group.com

Group resources actually work!

This Group resource helps you focus on **"The 1 Thing®"**—a life-changing relationship with Jesus Christ. "The 1 Thing" incorporates our **R.E.A.L.** approach to ministry. It reinforces a growing friendship with Jesus, encourages long-term learning, and results in life transformation, because it's:

Relational
Learner-to-learner interaction enhances learning and builds Christian friendships.

Experiential
What learners experience through discussion and action sticks with them up to 9 times longer than what they simply hear or read.

Applicable
The aim of Christian education is to equip learners to be both hearers and doers of God's Word.

Learner-based
Learners understand and retain more when the learning process takes into consideration how they learn best.

Group

GROUP'S BODY-BUILDING GUIDE TO COMMUNITY: STRENGTHENING RELATIONSHIPS IN YOUR CHURCH
Copyright © 2006 Group Publishing, Inc.

Visit our Web site: **www.group.com**

CREDITS

Writers: M. Scott Boren, Mikal Keefer, and Jennifer Root Wilger
Editor: Candace McMahan
Chief Creative Officer: Joani Schultz
Copy Editor: Amber Van Schooneveld
Art Director: Joey Rusk
Print Production Artists: Shelly Dillon and Julia Martin
Cover Art Director: Jeff A. Storm
Cover Designer: Veronica Lucas
Cover Photographer: Rodney Stewart
Production Manager: DeAnne Lear

Unless otherwise noted, Scripture taken from the HOLY BIBLE, NEW INTERNATIONAL VERSION®. Copyright © 1973, 1978, 1984 by International Bible Society. Used by permission of Zondervan Publishing House. All rights reserved.

LIBRARY OF CONGRESS CATALOGING-IN-PUBLICATION DATA

Group's body-building guide to community : strengthening relationships in your church.
    p. cm.
ISBN-13: 978-0-7644-2936-1 (pbk. : alk. paper)
1. Community--Religious aspects--Christianity. 2. Church work. 3. Church group work. 4. Small groups--Religious aspects--Christianity. 5. Fellowship--Religious aspects--Christianity. I. Group Publishing.
BV625.G68 2006
253--dc22

          2006012391

ISBN 0-7644-2936-1

10 9 8 7 6 5 4 3 2 1   15 14 13 12 11 10 09 08 07 06

Printed in the United States of America.

DEDICATION

"There should be no division in the body, but...its parts should have equal concern for each other. If one part suffers, every part suffers with it; if one part is honored, every part rejoices with it."
—1 Corinthians 12:25-26

To all of the people who work to build up the body of Christ and have so graciously shared their stories with us, we extend our deepest thanks. Special thanks to Stuart Bond, Lauren Brown, Lisa Burney, Stephanie and Steve Caro, Sandi Dillon, Jim Egli, Daryl Eldridge, Lyn Foote, Brad and Amy Gilliland, Jane Harlan, Jim Hawley, Carl Hofmann, Jeanette Holdridge, Barb Jacobson, Casey Keepers, Dave Kirkham, Anissa and Peter Lay, Olon M. Lindemood, Bryan Loritts, O'Dell Massey, Roy Miller, Linda Mohrman, Jan and Pat Reeder, Scott Riley, Greg Sanders, Mark Toone, and Jennifer and Tom Wilger.

—Group Publishing

C O N T E N T S

C O N T E N T S

I N T R O D U C T I O N

It's no secret that people are hungry for community, for a genuine sense of belonging, for the sure knowledge that they are deeply cared for beyond the circle of their immediate family. And it is this desire for community that draws many Christians as well as non-Christians to the church.

Yet in our culture, in which people scurry from one appointment, obligation, or event to another, community—even in the church—is harder and harder to find. As a church grows, it must become more and more intentional about finding ways to engender a sense of belonging, or before long its very growth will snuff out one flame that initially drew people to it. And smaller churches must also be intentional about ensuring that everyone—young and old, black and white, wealthy and poor—feels enfolded in the body of Christ.

Over the years churches have relied on many of the same methods for building and maintaining community, including potluck suppers, small groups, and prayer groups. All of these tried-and-true methods have worked, or they wouldn't have lasted as long as they have. But with time they may have become stale and lost some of their appeal.

If your church is looking for fresh ways to build community, delve into the pages of this book. In it you'll find innovative ideas that convey a deep sense of caring to every person in the church.

In Chapter 4, for example, you'll discover how one church has transformed an event traditionally known to actually *repel* members—the annual meeting—into the one church event that members won't miss.

In Chapter 3, you'll learn about a church in the South that works hard to bridge the chasm separating races to create an environment of growing trust and understanding, a place where members of all races feel equally at home.

In Chapter 2, you'll read about a large, downtown church that has put a new spin on the time-honored midweek church potluck—an event that is so magnetic it draws members away from their homes, television sets, and easy chairs in the middle of the week simply to enjoy a good meal in the company of people who love them.

You'll find ideas to build community between adults and children, and among men, among women of all ages, and among mothers of young children.

You'll find ways to let those who are no longer able to attend know that they're not forgotten: students who have gone away to college; people recovering from illness, childbirth, and surgery; and those who are no longer physically able to go to church.

You'll find community-building ideas that can be carried out individually and as an entire church body. Whether your church is large or small, long-established or just beginning, the churches profiled in this book will give you practical ways to demonstrate Jesus' love to everyone who enters its doors.

Few things are more appealing than being surrounded by loving people. This book will give you practical ways to make sure your church does just that.

CHAPTER ONE

BUILD COMMUNITY AMONG MEN

Large church, small church, *any* church can make "Guys' Movie Night" a relational, community-building part of its men's ministry.

- ☑ EASY TO IMPLEMENT
- ☑ WORKS FOR CHURCHES OF ANY SIZE
- ☑ BUILDS MEN'S MINISTRY
- ☑ PROMOTES SMALL GROUPS
- ☑ REQUIRES MINIMAL VOLUNTEER MANAGEMENT

GUYS' MOVIE NIGHT

Jim Hawley took a long look at the suburban house on his left as he pulled his car to the curb. It was Friday night, already growing dark, when Jim unfolded his lanky frame and double-checked the house address.

Jim was showing up to watch a movie with half a dozen other guys. No dates—just guys.

And Jim had absolutely no idea what movie he'd see. *That* detail was a deep secret known only to the guy hosting the first "GMN" (Guys' Movie Night) Jim attended.

"I'm not much of a joiner," Jim says. Yet he jumped at the chance to catch a movie with some other guys—especially since the invitation promised there would be time to discuss the film.

"When I see movies, I want to talk about them later—explore what the movie meant, what the director was trying to say, that sort of thing. When you see movies with other men, there's usually not much talking afterward."

Jim walked to the door, greeted the guys already there, and snagged a spot on the sofa. The movie was an oldie but goodie: *Kramer vs. Kramer*. When the movie ended, the host turned off the video player.

> **GMN GIVES MEN THE CHANCE TO SORT OUT ISSUES BY TALKING ABOUT THEM WITH OTHER MEN. THAT'S SOMETHING THAT DOESN'T OFTEN HAPPEN AT CHURCH.**
> —JIM HAWLEY

"*That's* when it got interesting," remembers Jim. "*Kramer vs. Kramer* is all about a marriage falling apart. It turns out we'd all been touched by divorce somehow—either our own or our parents'. The discussion got past the surface pretty fast, with guys sharing what they'd been through and how divorce had affected them.

"We talked until midnight, and, somewhere in the process, that group became a small faith community," Jim says.

For Jim, who was emerging from some disappointing church experiences, Guys' Movie Night was a healing experience. "*That* was the kind of community I wanted and needed," he says. "Someplace I could say what I thought and not be judged for it. Someplace I could tell my story."

Jim hasn't missed a GMN since. He's even hosted a few at his place.

Guys getting together to stare at a television screen is nothing new—the National Football League couldn't survive without it—but seldom has a television screen been part of a community-building strategy.

And, at least for some guys, that's a shame.

"Watching and then discussing thought-provoking movies is a safe way for men to talk about faith," says Jim. "Guys can share their stuff indirectly, talking about the characters in the movie. It's a springboard to more personal discussions."

Of course, not *every* movie is an appropriate discussion starter (more about that later), but there's no shortage of movies that are perfect for a Guys' Movie Night. And if asked, there's no shortage of guys willing to attend.

A BACK DOOR TO COMMUNITY

A Guys' Movie Night is a low-commitment launchpad for building relationships among men. Guys who attend aren't required to talk unless they want to, although most are comfortable enough to enter into discussion.

Think of a GMN as a threshold community-building experience for men. It's a place men can stick their toes into the shallow end of the relational pool before diving into deep water. For Jim Hawley, the group of guys who met to watch a movie became more than buddies. They became a community of brothers.

"You might not think a movie experience would be any deeper than getting together to watch a baseball game," he says. "But there have been deep, deep moments of sharing."

And Jim discovered an additional benefit: "I always went home and told my wife about what we'd seen and what I'd discovered. She and I usually ended up renting the same movie and watching it together so we could talk about it, too."

LAUNCHING A GUYS' MOVIE NIGHT IN YOUR CHURCH

The most important thing to remember in launching a GMN is that the point *isn't* to watch movies. The point is to stimulate discussion and encourage fellowship. The movies are simply shared experiences designed to prompt discussions.

This isn't the sort of program your church can replicate on a grand scale by announcing a congregation-wide Guys' Movie Night and setting up a popcorn machine in the back of the sanctuary. Guys will stay away in droves, and you'll probably break federal copyright laws the moment you fire up the video player.

This is an *organic*, grass-roots program that spreads as networks of guys discover that it's a good thing to have guy friends. That the meetings are safe places to express themselves and discover what their friends think and believe. That they're not alone.

Want to start a Guys' Movie Night in your church? Do it with a whisper, not with fanfare. Suggest to several of the more social men in your church that they give it a try, and pass along the information in this chapter. Ask the men to consider inviting not only their church buddies, but non-Christian friends as well.

Then walk away. Leave it alone. It'll either grow wings and fly, or it will never get off the ground.

Jim's GMN has been meeting quarterly for years with attendance ranging from six to 15. There's no formal membership, and guys rotate in and out depending on jobs, relocations, and schedules. Just recently Jim himself moved several states away.

"I thought about starting a Guys' Movie Night where I live now," says Jim, who quickly discovered he didn't have to. "My church has a similar program going, so I've just joined it," he says.

Jim's church believes in engaging with current culture, so movie selection tends to be more current (and therefore less readily available on video or DVD). Church members catch a movie at a local theater and then filter what they've seen and heard through their understanding of Scripture and their experience as Christians. That leads to lively—and faith-shaping—discussions at local restaurants after the shows.

Still, Jim misses the intimacy of hanging with guy friends in someone's home. He still speaks warmly of his GMN experience.

"I think it's just a matter of time before I get something going here," he says.

When Jim's ready, he'll invite six or seven guys to come over to his house on a Friday night. And he'll get his Guys' Movie Night off on the right foot by incorporating 10 principles learned in his previous group...

NO WOMEN ALLOWED

This event is exclusive to men. When hosting a GMN, guys who are married remind their wives not drop in to watch the movie. Most wives actually leave the house.

This policy allows for deeper, more honest discussions among the men who attend.

MEET IN HOMES

This is smart for several reasons, one being the need to market the experience to wives.

It's one thing for a married guy to say, "Honey, I'm going to catch a movie with friends and then stop for dessert and discussion afterward." It's another thing to say, "Honey, me and some guys from church are watching a movie in Bubba's basement while we guzzle root beer and choke down beef jerky."

The theater option is something wives might actually want to *do* with their husbands. But you couldn't *pay* most wives to sit in a basement eating processed food while watching a video picked by someone named Bubba.

Meeting in homes also keeps the cost of hosting a GMN reasonable. All that's required is the cost of a video or DVD rental, snacks, and steam cleaning the carpet after someone spills a bowl of chili-cheese dip.

Besides, when men are invited into one another's homes, a bond forms. Call it the "brotherhood of the basement."

It's important to rotate hosts and homes, even if Stephen has a fully integrated surround-sound home theater system with plasma screen and Ryan has a 13-inch TV with vertical hold issues. When guys host the event, they're more invested and more likely to stay involved.

DON'T MEET TOO OFTEN

Every two to three months seems about right. If you meet more frequently, GMNs eat into guys' family time. If you meet less often, budding relationships lose momentum.

Don't let a GMN end without nailing down a host for the next GMN. Give the next host 90 days to select a movie, pick a Friday night, and host the event.

SERVE ONLY BASIC GUY FOOD

Ask men to bring food from the four basic guy food groups: fat, caffeine, sugar, and barbecue sauce. A quarterly movie night isn't the place to sweat calories or a balanced diet.

Having each attendee bring something to pass around is one more way to build ownership of the event.

PG OR PG-13 ONLY, PLEASE

There are dozens of engaging, thoughtful, discussion-sparking movies in the PG to PG-13 range. Short of screening *Bambi* repeatedly, there will be something in each movie that offends someone—but a PG-13 rating usually ensures that the offense will be minor.

A related word of advice: Forget forwarding past "bad" scenes or selectively muting the soundtrack. No one's that quick on the trigger, and censorship destroys the viewing experience. It's better to not screen a movie than to attempt to clean it up.

KEEP THE MOVIE TITLE SECRET

Announcing the title in advance tempts guys to attend or skip a Guys' Movie Night based on whether they've already seen the film.

Remember, *the movie isn't the point*. When men discuss what they've seen, even a familiar movie takes on new meaning. The time to announce the movie title is when guys' plates are full of chicken wings and everyone's parked in front of the screen.

CHOOSE MOVIES WISELY

A winning strategy is to let whoever hosts a Guys' Movie Night select the film to be screened. Pressure? You bet—but it builds enormous personal commitment to guaranteeing the selection is a good one.

Another suggestion: Set some standards. Jim's group has put the following criteria in place.

Movies must be...

- **PG-13 or tamer—unless there's a *very* good reason.** Some PG-13 movies contain more sexual content than R movies that feature on-screen shooting. Guys in Jim's group didn't care about language and occasional violence; sexually explicit situations are the greater concern. And while ratings aren't a guarantee, they do help avoid overtly sexual content.

- **prescreened by the host *before* being shown to the group.** What a guy remembers from a movie and what is actually there can vary tremendously. Avoid "Oops—I forgot about that scene" moments.

- **less than two and a half hours long.** Leave time for discussion. Try to draw the line at two hours.

- **thought-provoking and have spiritual and/or emotional content.** A guy in Jim's group once screened an art-house film, and when the lights came up, confessed, "I don't really know why I picked that movie." The ensuing discussion started out slow and then fizzled altogether.

- **films most guys probably haven't seen, at least lately.** That knocks out anything in the "new release" section of the video store.

These filters effectively weed out recent blockbusters, as well as racier movies. The good news is that there are still *lots* of options. Guys in Jim's group have brought in "little films" that never saw national distribution in major theaters. Sometimes films created for HBO and other cable channels are excellent choices, though they're often not rated and require careful prescreening.

Guys who are *really* brave show "chick flicks." This genre focuses on relationships and provides great discussion material. It also tends to prompt comments such as "That *You've Got Mail* movie would've been better if Tom Hanks had just blown up Meg Ryan's bookstore in the first place."

NO PAUSING

Once the movie starts, it keeps rolling. If guys have to visit the little boys room, they step out and miss a few minutes of the film or hold it and do their business later.

THE HOST CONTROLS THE REMOTE

This is a matter of respect. Guys don't go into another man's home and kick his dog, do they? Then why would they think they could touch his remote?

THE HOST LAUNCHES THE DISCUSSION

After the movie ends, it's the host's job to get the conversation rolling. The discussion may take a dramatic turn once it starts, but the first nudge is up to the host.

For instance, after *Apollo 13* ends the host might say, "How calm do you think we'd be knowing we were about to die? What does that say about what we believe happens after death?" The discussion may eventually center on the way people react when under pressure at work—but the host got things going.

Three suggestions about leading a movie-night discussion:

1. **Don't let anyone dominate the conversation.** This can happen in several ways, so look for these personality types:
   - The *therapist* is very comfortable with opening up (or expecting others to do so) in a group setting. This person may confuse the movie night with group therapy. He'll want to explore deep, personal issues at length and share poignant stories that illustrate his inner conflict. This will, of course, freak out the other guys and send them screaming for the door.

     Gently let therapists know that while conversation at a GMN can—and should—dip beneath the surface, few men show up expecting to scuba dive in emotional waters.
   - The *evangelist* always looks for a way to bring the discussion back to a need for Christ. While this isn't a bad thing in itself, making a faith decision isn't the point of *The Truman Show*.

     Remind evangelists that GMN is about forming relationships and building community. It's the growing relationships that give men permission to speak truth into each other's lives.
   - The *jokester* isn't comfortable with getting personal, so he turns every comment into a punch line. Eventually, this will shut down

conversation. Who wants to share anything when there's a good chance he'll be harpooned by a joke?

Refuse to play the jokester's game. Gently challenge the jokester's behavior—even pulling him aside to discuss it if necessary. Don't let conversation be shut down by his humor. If the jokes are creating silences rather than community, distancing rather than drawing men closer, consider the humor a cancer that must be addressed before it kills your discussions.

2. **Ask follow-up and personal questions.**

If Jack says he thinks Mr. Holland (in *Mr. Holland's Opus*) sold out for a paycheck instead of starving until becoming a famous composer, you might ask, "How important is it to do something significant?" If Jack says it's important, gently probe further by personalizing the next question: "What accomplishment would feel significant for you? What do you want to accomplish before you die?"

> **"GREAT QUESTIONS THAT TAKE A DISCUSSION TO THE HEART OF THE MATTER AREN'T AN INTRUSION—THEY'RE A GIFT. ASK THEM. "**
> —JIM HAWLEY

3. **Set ground rules.** After a few GMNs, a group develops a rhythm for discussions. Still, it never hurts to establish a few ground rules and occasionally review expectations. Here are some to consider:
   - This is a *group* discussion. Leave room for everyone to comment.
   - It's OK to disagree but not to be disagreeable. Every point of view will be respected.
   - No double dipping in the salsa.

That pretty much covers it. After ground rules have been set, group discussions will be self-governing. Men will challenge each other's comments—but not in a demeaning or critical way.

A BONUS INSIGHT—KEEP THIS ONE TO YOURSELF

When your church launches a Guys' Movie Night and you end up hosting, here's a question that *always* works when a discussion is floundering: "Which character in this movie do you most closely identify with—and why?" Tuck that question in your wallet next to your emergency $20 bill, and don't pull it out until you're truly desperate.

THE MOVIES

Following is a starter list of three films with accompanying discussion starters. Each has been used at a Guys' Movie Night and worked well.

The Apostle (1997)

Genre: Drama

Length: 134 minutes

Rating: PG-13 for thematic elements and a related scene of violence

Plot: "Sonny" Dewey is a Texas preacher who discovers his beautiful wife is having an affair with Horace, a younger minister. After assaulting Horace, Sonny disappears and starts over in Louisiana. He leaves his life behind but not his faith. This movie chronicles Sonny's path to redemption and his confrontation with his past.

Discussion Starters

- Is the statement "Sonny was a faithful Christian" true or false? Why do you answer as you do?
- In what way does Sonny's faith journey remind you of your own?
- If you were able to pass sentence on Sonny when he's brought to trial back in Texas, what sentence would you give? Why?

Galaxy Quest (1999)

Genre: Action/Adventure/Comedy

Length: 102 minutes

Rating: PG for action violence, mild language, and sensuality

Plot: When cast members of a long-cancelled television show discover they've been taken seriously by a race of aliens, they get the chance to play out their TV roles in real life—and the stakes are high.

Discussion Starters

- Describe a time you felt like a fraud—when you felt less competent than people assumed you were. What happened? How did it turn out?
- How does it feel when people express confidence in you?
- How does it feel when people express confidence in you but they clearly *don't* have confidence in you?
- When it comes to living out what we believe, is it a good thing to act confident about our religious beliefs even if we're feeling doubt inside? Why or why not?

October Sky (1999)

Genre: Drama

Length: 108 minutes

Rating: PG for language, brief teen sensuality, alcohol use, and some thematic elements

Plot: Nothing in the coal-mining town where Homer Hickam was raised encouraged scientific experimentation. So Homer's desire to build and test rockets is met with...well, a distinct lack of enthusiasm. Homer and several friends are determined to build a viable rocket and win scholarships through a science fair.

Discussion Starters

- What have you wanted to do so much that you were willing to risk ridicule and failure?
- What's a dream you've had that you were willing to work hard to make real?
- Describe a time you stuck with something that was difficult. What was it? What happened?

FINAL THOUGHTS ABOUT...CONFIDENTIALITY

If you want men to share what they *really* think and feel about sensitive issues, a level of confidentiality must be maintained. Especially if you have guys who float in and out of the group, be intentional about saying it before each discussion: What's said at GMN stays at GMN. Make it clear that the only exception is if a participant reveals he's about to hurt himself or others or do something illegal.

And don't be discouraged if in your church of 150 there are only half a dozen guys who participate in a GMN. Any entry into community is valuable, and GMNs appeal to men who might find no other door into that place of safety, friendship, and spiritual growth.

> "AS IRON SHARPENS IRON, SO ONE MAN SHARPENS ANOTHER."
> —PROVERBS 27:17

BUILD COMMUNITY
THROUGH A NEW TAKE
ON MEAL MINISTRY

A large, downtown church builds community across the
generations by putting a modern spin on the time-honored
midweek church potluck.

☑ WORKS FOR CHURCHES OF ANY SIZE

☑ FOSTERS INTERGENERATIONAL COMMUNITY

☑ REQUIRES GOOD VOLUNTEER MANAGEMENT

A BIG BATCH OF PEOPLE

First Presbyterian Church of Boulder, Colorado, is a big church. In a denomination where the mean church size is 214, First Pres reports a weekly worship attendance of over 1,500. Being a big church has its benefits: in this case dynamic worship services, a talented pastoral staff, a thriving youth ministry, and a recently renovated children's wing, to name just a few. But being a big church also has its challenges. In a sea of 1,500 faces, how do people make connections? In the shifting tide between worship services, it's sometimes hard to move, much less carry on a conversation. Sometimes a big church is just so, well, big.

How can a big church be made to feel smaller and more like a community? This is the question that laid the foundation for the Bible Bistro program at First Presbyterian Church. The church had already identified community building as a priority in its ministry master plan. It had created and budgeted for an associate pastor position to oversee community life. But for many months, the position remained unfilled. Something was needed to fill the gap while the church waited for the right person to fill the position. After much reflection, the church leadership decided to begin with the familiar: a midweek dinner followed by a new adult education class, Discipleship 101.

A NEW RECIPE FOR COMMUNITY

"The original thinking behind the Bistro was to provide a weekly community-building event for the church family while we waited for the associate pastor of community life," explains Carl Hofmann, associate pastor of spiritual formation and discipleship at First Pres. "The motto 'help make a big church feel smaller' (which characterized the position description) was our goal for the Wednesday night dinner and class to follow. It made sense to try Wednesdays because so many groups were already meeting that night, and we would not have to drag families out for an additional night during the week."

Indeed, First Pres was already bustling on Wednesday nights. Upstairs, elementary-aged children planned and carried out service projects for the church and community. Downstairs, swelling ranks of middle and high school students swarmed through the building. Families were definitely coming and going, but not necessarily together. As the plans came together for the Bible Bistro program, Carl and his Adult Christian Education (ACE) team hoped that the dinners would create a comfortable time and space for families to sit down, relax, and enjoy friends and fellowship before going their separate ways.

It was an ambitious project, even (and maybe especially) for a big church. The thought of rounding up enough volunteers to serve dinner every week was daunting in itself. With everything else going on, meeting (and eating) space was somewhat scarce. The church kitchen was spacious, but it was limited in its functionality by poor design and aging equipment. Nevertheless, the team decided to go forward and began publicizing the idea over the summer in advance of a September kickoff.

PRIMING THE POT

The Bible Bistro concept intrigued many in the congregation, including Tom and Jennifer Wilger. Both enjoyed cooking and were looking for ways to practice their gifts of hospitality and administration. In addition, Jennifer had grown up in a smaller church where regular Wednesday night dinners were the norm. She recalls, "In those days, most of the meals were prepared by 'the little church ladies,' as we teenagers liked to refer to them. The food was horrible, but still almost everybody came. It was a great time for people of all ages to socialize."

At first, the Wilgers simply resolved that they would attend the Bistro dinners. But when Jennifer saw the blurb in the Sunday bulletin inviting church members with culinary abilities to inquire about serving in the Bistro ministry, she urged Tom to look into it with her. Tom agreed, hoping with her that a Wednesday night "bistro" dinner would foster the great fellowship she remembered, but with better food.

❝WE'RE CHANGING THE TASTE OF CHURCH COOKING... ONE WEDNESDAY AT A TIME!❞
—JENNIFER WILGER

A few short weeks and several phone calls later, the couple had a meeting with Carl Hofmann, Senior Pastor Peter Barnes, and Church Business Manager Bob Stover to discuss the details. To set the stage for this important conversation about food ministry, the Wilgers prepared a lunch of grilled chicken Caesar salad and homemade focaccia. As they enjoyed the meal, the group discussed the desired ambiance of the Bible Bistro. All agreed it should provide a quality dining experience, not unlike what people would find in the many restaurants within walking distance of the church. In addition to the food, the bistro feel would be achieved through simple, classic table décor, live music, and a friendly, unobtrusive emcee. Based on previous attempts at a midweek dinner, the Wilgers were told to expect 60 to 80 people to attend.

SIMMERING...

Tom and Jennifer settled on spinach lasagna for the first dinner, as it was easy to prepare, vegetarian-friendly, and seemed like a manageable dish to scale up for a large group. It also seemed like something most kids might eat. But Jennifer's experience as a mom and preschool teacher led her to develop a few special menu items just for younger children.

"As a mom, I know that keeping kids happy can make or break any mealtime experience," Jennifer reflected. "When restaurants go out of their way to offer food that's fun for kids, I remember that—and I go back. We want families to want to eat here." So Wilger made it a point to offer kid-friendly, healthy finger foods such as baby carrots, cheese sticks, and mini-bagels at a special kids' table. She also obtained high chairs and booster seats so families with babies and toddlers could comfortably enjoy their meals. She even prepared simple, homemade baby food (puréed apples or squash).

After finalizing all the menu items, the Wilgers met with the ACE team to discuss logistics. A volunteer coordinator from ACE agreed to recruit workers for the first few dinners. Arrangements were made to have a cash box and receipts for people's payments. A recorded message was set up to receive registrations by phone.

As the Bistro kickoff grew closer, reservation numbers continued to rise. The Wilgers wondered how many lasagnas it would take to serve 100 people. What about 120 people? 150? And what about volunteer help? Who would serve all these people? As the preparations continued, Jennifer prayed for peace. Although slightly unnerved by the growing size of the Bistro, the Wilgers trusted that the rising numbers indicated the program would truly be meeting a need.

SERVING UP CONNECTIONS

When the day of the first Bistro dinner finally arrived, 185 people attended. The program sustained an attendance of over 100 for its first 10 weeks, and then dropped off to the expected 60 to 80 the following semester. Despite the reduced attendance, the team refused to be discouraged. In a large church full of very busy people, few events outside of Sunday worship are attended by 50 or more. And for those who attended, the meal *was* meeting a need.

"I love the Bible Bistro," says Lauren Brown, a college student who attended. "The Bible Bistro is one of the main reasons I decided to join this church.

> THE CHURCH IS PERHAPS ONE OF THE FEW PLACES LEFT WHERE WE CAN MEET PEOPLE WHO ARE DIFFERENT THAN WE ARE BUT WITH WHOM WE CAN FORM A LARGER FAMILY.
> —HENRI NOUWEN

I believe church should be a multigenerational experience, and that is what the Bible Bistro did. It brought together people from every part of the church, sharing a meal together. Instead of hanging out with just my friends, I'd end up at a table with seven assorted people, doing something we all have to do, eat. As a college student and new member, it really helped me feel a part of the church."

In addition to the fellowship she experienced over the meal, Lauren enjoyed serving as a regular Bistro volunteer. "I met so many people," she recalls. "I was setting tables with little kids, single moms, and senior citizens. I never would have met all those people just by sitting in church on Sundays."

Pat and Jan Reeder attended regularly with their grown son and his family. "We came for the [Discipleship 101] class," Pat explained, "but we had a lot of fun helping with the meal. It helped us meet people and find a way of serving in the church." Jennifer echoes the Reeders' experience. "I didn't realize how unconnected we were. Before the Bistro, we pretty much came and went to church anonymously. Now we know people. The regular Bistro volunteers and attendees are now a large part of our community."

After the first 10 weeks of Bible Bistro, the ACE team reconvened to debrief the experience. The "experiment" in community building was deemed a grand success. Carl Hofmann commented, "We've heard nothing but enthusiastic feedback from participants...Clearly our congregation is hungry for connections and deeper fellowship." Post-Bistro written surveys completed by the first set of participants confirmed the positive reception, with comments such as "Just wonderful food and companionship," and "We love the intergenerational aspect of this dinner."

The Bible Bistro continued at First Presbyterian for a year and a half. At this writing, the program is on hiatus. The church has hired an associate pastor of community life, and she is in the process of getting to know the congregation and determining which programs will best meet the church's felt need for community. The church is also in the midst of evaluating a large remodeling project, which, among other things, would involve demolishing and renovating the existing church kitchen. The Wilgers remain involved in meal ministry at First Presbyterian and regularly oversee meal preparation for other churchwide community-building events.

CHAPTER TWO

IMPLEMENTATION

HOW YOUR CHURCH CAN BEGIN A MEAL MINISTRY

STEPS TO TAKE

1. Discuss the idea with your congregation. Identify potential times that meal ministry could be worked into the life of your church community.
2. Choose a person, couple, or group to coordinate your meal program. Ideally, the coordinator(s) should have a passion for hospitality, a love of good food, and experience in cooking for large groups.

> **Staffing**
>
> *Coordinating a weekly meal program is a lot of work! In addition to the actual cooking, the meal coordinator is responsible for menu planning, shopping, and volunteer management. If possible, consider hiring someone for this task. To serve up to 50 people, plan on at least 10 hours per week at an hourly rate of $10 to $15. This cost can be folded into the price of the meal.*

3. Recruit volunteers to help cook, serve, and clean up after the meals. Sample volunteer job descriptions may be found on pages 28-30.
4. Publicize the program. Include times, dates, and meal prices. (Be realistic in meal pricing. Unless your church can budget additional money for a meal program, the price people pay to eat should cover what it costs to provide the meal, including food, paper goods, and the coordinator's time.)
5. Welcome the hungry hordes, and savor the sweet smells of community!

LESSONS LEARNED

As the Bistro evolved, the Wilgers visited other churches with established meal programs. The following ideas helped shape the Bible Bistro and can help you as you consider a meal program for your church.

1. Offer a meal in conjunction with an established church program. People are more likely to incorporate a church meal into their busy schedules if it is offered at a time they'd be coming to church anyway.

2. Match your meal to your mission. If convenience is part of your goal, try grab-and-go sandwiches. If you want people to linger around the tables, serve the food family style.

3. Don't forget to surround your ministry with prayer. Ask God to break down any barriers that might prevent people from entering into true community as a result of your program.

FINAL THOUGHTS ABOUT...COOKING WITH JESUS

Jennifer Wilger says, "When we first started cooking for Bible Bistro, a lady in the church spent an hour showing us around the church kitchen. She pointed out all of the flaws in the kitchen, handed over a dilapidated copy of *Food for Fifty*, and wished us well. 'When you're cooking with Jesus,' she said, 'a lot of little miracles happen.'"

"As we prepared for the first Bistro dinner, we needed 13 giant cans of tomatoes. Costco! Guess what? No canned tomatoes of any kind at Costco that day. But at the neighborhood grocery store, in the quarter of an aisle devoted to bulk foods, there were exactly 13 cans of tomatoes. That was only the first of many 'little miracles' that constantly reminded us that if our ministry was effective, it was because we were 'cooking with Jesus.'"

"SHARED MEALS ARE CENTRAL TO EVERY COMMUNITY OF HOSPITALITY—CENTRAL TO SUSTAINING THE LIFE OF THE COMMUNITY AND TO EXPRESSING WELCOME TO STRANGERS."
—CHRISTINE D. POHL

BIBLE BISTRO KITCHEN VOLUNTEER JOBS

First Presbyterian used the following job descriptions for Bible Bistro volunteers. Feel free to adapt them to your church's needs.

Volunteers

If finding regular weekly volunteers proves challenging, try this Bible Bistro recruitment tip: Invite different ministries or small groups to staff the meal each week. Depending on your church size, each group will need to volunteer only once or twice per semester. In addition to spending time with each other, ministry groups will meet new people and expose others to their areas of service.

Task: Beverages

Volunteers needed: 1 to 2

Time: 30 minutes prior to serving

1. Locate two pitchers for each table (one for water, one for iced tea or punch).

2. Fill the water pitchers two-thirds full of cold water.

3. If tea or punch is being served, mix the beverage as instructed; then fill the pitchers two-thirds full.

4. When people begin to sit at the tables, add ice to the water pitchers, and set them on the tables (usually 15 minutes before serving).

5. Ten minutes before serving, add ice to the tea or punch, and set the pitchers on the tables.

6. Prepare additional punch or tea in a large mixing container to use for refills.

7. Monitor beverage consumption, and refill pitchers as needed.

Task: Bread

Volunteers needed: 1

Time: 15 to 20 minutes prior to serving

1. Line bread baskets with towels.

2. Put eight to 10 slices of bread in each basket, and cover with a towel.

3. Place extra bread (if any) in large baskets, and cover with towels.

4. Shortly before serving begins, set a basket of bread on each table.

5. If extra bread is available, monitor bread consumption, and refill baskets or offer individual slices as needed.

Task: Dishes

Volunteers needed: 2 to 4

Time: Anytime!

1. Fill sink with hot, soapy water.

2. Rinse food residue from dishes. Run disposal as needed.

3. Stack rinsed dishes to be washed on counter.

4. Wash, rinse, and sanitize dishes (if sanitizing equipment is available).

5. Set clean dishes to be dried on counter.

6. Dry dishes, and put them away in their proper places. If you can't find the right place for something, ask!

Task: Kids Table

Volunteers needed: 1 to 2

Time: 30 minutes prior to serving

1. Set out kids' plates.

2. Set out baby food containers.

3. Put baby carrots on ice in a serving bowl. Set out baby carrots (with serving tongs or spoon) and ranch dressing.

4. Pour applesauce in a bowl. Set out applesauce with a serving spoon.

5. Check with coordinator for any additional food items.

6. Help kids and parents serve food at serving time. Monitor portion sizes and second helpings (not until everyone has been through the line) as needed.

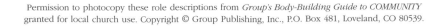

Task: Salad

Volunteers needed: 1 to 2

Time: 30 to 60 minutes prior to serving

1. Wash and dry salad greens.

2. Deliver colander and salad spinner to dishwashing area.

3. Cut or tear lettuce leaves if needed.

4. Cut up additional salad items as needed.

5. Place an equal amount of salad greens in large, plastic salad bowls.

6. Divide additional salad items equally between the bowls of salad greens.

7. Put salads in refrigerator.

8. Ten minutes before serving time, dress and toss all but one or two of the complete salads.

9. Monitor salad consumption. Remove empty salad bowls, and deliver to dishwashing area.

10. If needed, add dressing to remaining salad(s). Toss and set out on serving table.

Task: Food Server

Volunteers needed: 4 to 5

Time: 30 minutes prior to serving

1. Arrive in time to hear menu review, including ingredients (in case diners have questions about allergies or special diets) and portion sizes.

2. Cut main dish into serving portions if needed.

3. Serve main dish or salad/side dish to people as they come through the line. Be prepared to answer questions about the food.

4. When food pans are two-thirds empty, request more food from the kitchen.

5. Deliver empty food pans to the dishwashing area.

6. When everyone has gone through the line, inform people if more food is available for second helpings.

Task: Dessert Server (if needed)

Volunteers needed: 1 to 2 (can also be food servers)

Time: Serving time or before

1. Cut dessert into serving-size portions.

2. Place servings on plates.

3. Deliver desserts to the tables.

4. Deliver empty dessert pans to the dishwashing area.

SAMPLE RECIPE

You can find recipes for church meals from many different sources. *Food for Fifty* and other similar cookbooks provide large-quantity recipes, or you can scale up recipes from your own cookbooks or files. You can find 12x20-inch baking pans in many church kitchens and at restaurant-supply stores. These fit in a standard-size oven and generally serve 18 to 24 people, depending on the type of food. When scaling your own recipes, keep in mind that one 12x20-inch pan is approximately equal to two 9x13-inch pans.

Chicken Pot Pie Filling

One 12x20-inch pan

Serves 18

This traditional pot pie filling may be enhanced by additional fresh vegetables but can also be prepared simply with onions, carrots, and celery. The biscuit-dough topping is easier to handle in large quantities than pie crust.

For a vegetarian version, substitute vegetable broth, leave out the chicken, and add as many veggies as your budget will allow.

3 pounds boneless, skinless chicken breasts

4 cups chicken broth (one 32-ounce carton)

3 tablespoons vegetable oil

1 to 2 onions, diced (if you're making multiple pans, figure 1 onion per pan)

4 to 6 medium carrots, peeled and chopped

4 stalks celery, diced

1 red pepper, seeded and diced

salt and pepper to taste

1 stick unsalted butter

1 cup flour

3 cups milk

1 teaspoon dried thyme or rosemary (or 1 tablespoon finely chopped fresh)

¼ cup dry sherry or white wine (optional)

2 cups frozen green peas, corn, or a combination, thawed

1/3 cup fresh parsley, chopped

purchased or prepared biscuit dough, enough for 18 or more biscuits

UP TO TWO DAYS AHEAD

1. Place the chicken and broth in a large stockpot. Cover, bring to a simmer, and cook until the chicken is just done, 8-10 minutes. (Remember, it will also be baked in the oven, so it's better to undercook it slightly than to overcook it!)
2. Transfer the cooked chicken to a bowl. Transfer the broth to a bowl and save it for later.
3. Heat the vegetable oil in the same pot. Add the onions, carrots, celery, and red pepper. Sauté until just tender. Season with salt and pepper to taste. Remove from the pot and set aside.
4. Shred the now-cooled chicken, and combine with the vegetables in a large bowl. Refrigerate until needed.

UP TO ONE DAY AHEAD

1. Melt the butter over medium heat in the same pot. Gradually stir in the flour; then cook for about one minute. Using a whisk, mix in the reserved chicken broth, milk, and thyme or rosemary. Cook to desired thickness. *If you are cooking more than two pans, you will need to add more flour gradually and allow plenty of time (up to half an hour or more) for thickening.*
2. Salt and pepper to taste; then stir in the sherry or white wine, if using.
3. Pour the sauce over the chicken and vegetables; then stir in the peas or corn and parsley.

Note: If you choose to stagger the preparation, gently reheat the filling before continuing. For multiple pans of filling, allow up to an hour or more for reheating.

ON THE DAY OF THE MEAL

1. Spray a 12x20-inch pan with nonstick cooking spray. (If you neglect to do this, your cleanup volunteers may abandon you!)
2. Pour the warm filling into the pan.
3. Top with individual biscuits (3 rows of 6 or more biscuits per row, depending on biscuit size) or strips of biscuit dough. (Biscuit dough can be prepared and cut up to one day in advance.)
4. Bake at 400 degrees until biscuits are browned and filling is bubbly, 30 minutes or more. (If the biscuits brown before the filling is completely hot, cover the pan with aluminum foil.)

VARIATIONS

- Add or substitute other fresh vegetables: asparagus in the spring, green beans in the summer, butternut squash in the fall, and turnips or potatoes in the winter.
- Vary the herbs: Try basil with green beans, sage with butternut squash, or tarragon with asparagus.

BUILD COMMUNITY THROUGH RACIAL RECONCILIATION

This church has discovered a practical strategy that helps people participate in racial reconciliation.

- ☑ GREAT FOR RACIALLY DIVERSE CHURCHES
- ☑ INITIATES LONG-TERM INTERACTION
- ☑ REQUIRES LITTLE PREPARATION
- ☑ WORKS FOR CHURCHES OF ANY SIZE

A RADICAL STRATEGY

Memphis, Tennessee, is not known for its racial harmony. In fact, it is one of the most segregated cities in America. It is the city in which Martin Luther King Jr. was assassinated. It is certainly not a place most people would consider ripe for racial reconciliation. But Bryan Loritts is not like most people.

> **THERE IS NO DIFFERENCE BETWEEN JEW AND GENTILE—THE SAME LORD IS LORD OF ALL AND RICHLY BLESSES ALL WHO CALL ON HIM.**
> —ROMANS 10:12

Bryan and his young family moved to Memphis in 2003 with the goal of starting a church that would manifest a radical kingdom mindset by bringing blacks and whites together and bridging the chasm separating them. Bryan knows that without this kind of bridge-building, true harmony and unity in the body of Christ aren't possible. Thus began Fellowship Church. It started with 26 people and now is the church home of over 500 worshippers, both black and white.

A REALISTIC VISIONARY

Bryan is a black man with a radical vision, and he seeks to lead others to share this vision. But Bryan is also realistic. He knows he must provide simple steps for people to take before they will fully share his belief that racial reconciliation is attainable.

He therefore began to search for a way to help people overcome obstacles to interracial understanding. He realized he needed to create a safe place—a place where people can talk about issues that no one talks about, tough issues like stereotypes and prejudices, the kind of things that "nice" Christians don't verbalize even though they might think them.

THE IDEA IS BORN

To create this safe place, Bryan developed a four-week small-group experience called Erace groups. The purpose is "to facilitate a safe environment for people to be vulnerable and engage in discussion, with the hope of gaining a better understanding and appreciation of the perspective of another culture."

Bryan admits, "These groups will not solve the problems that divide the races, but they do provide a safe place to talk." At the very least, they initiate honest dialogue. In fact, they are designed with this specific goal in mind.

Each group is composed of 12 people—six of them are white; six are black. During the small-group experience, they are encouraged to verbalize their inner thoughts and feelings toward people of the other race. For example, during the first meeting, the facilitator asks group members to share at least three stereotypical ideas they have about people of a different race. At one meeting a white woman took a risk and said, "I see black men as the most promiscuous people on the planet."

While this kind of honesty can be offensive, it is common—and encouraged—in these groups. Bryan helps participants understand that the only way an Erace group will work is if its members are brutally honest. He writes in the syllabus, "Honesty and communication are valued over not wanting to look or sound silly or racist. We have to talk!" Bryan is adamant that the only way for people to overcome the things that divide them is to talk about them.

ERACE GROUND RULES

The primary ground rule is that **every subject is on the table.** This is an immersion experience, one that is based on a willingness to be completely transparent, at the risk of sounding stupid or mean, around the issue of race. Any fear of looking like a racist will only impede the process.

The second ground rule is that **everyone's input is necessary.** If even one group member withholds his or her thoughts or perspective, the group will not work.

This leads to the third ground rule: **When people do share their thoughts, they must be allowed to do so without fear of being attacked by those with a different point of view.** Again, they must be given the freedom to reveal what they think without fear, or the process won't work.

Bryan works hard to help other Christians understand that healthy conflict is OK. In fact, Bryan is convinced that it is this kind of conflict that will ultimately overcome interracial friction. The point of Erace groups is to talk things out, seek understanding, and clarify perspectives; with a topic as emotionally charged as this, conflict is inevitable. The key is to make sure it remains healthy.

The final ground rule is that **attendance at all four meetings is mandatory.** Bryan writes in the syllabus, "Because we have only four weeks together, attendance is a must. We need everyone to make sure they can attend all the meetings. If you cannot attend one of them, please let the facilitator know, and you will probably be asked to shift to another group at another time."

THE COMPOSITION OF THE GROUP

Bryan believes that the composition of the groups is crucial to their success, and he is very deliberate in his choice of participants. His overriding goal is to create an experience that will force people to deal with issues they would otherwise ignore.

Twelve is the maximum number in each group. Half must be white, and half must black. (This is because the congregation of Fellowship Church is primarily white and black. Other churches might be made up of groups such as Asians or Hispanics.)

In order to ensure that the group concentrates only on issues of race, Bryan selects people on the same socio-economic level. Otherwise, the issues become too complicated to address.

At the same time, he finds that the groups work best when they are multigenerational. Young professionals don't have firsthand knowledge of the assassination of Martin Luther King Jr., nor did they attend segregated schools. To hear stories from those who actually lived through these events is enlightening.

THE FACILITATOR

Currently, Bryan leads the Erace groups at Fellowship Church. He knows that the key to the success of these groups lies first in the ability of the facilitator to create a safe environment.

Once that is accomplished, Bryan describes his job as "finding the hot buttons and camping out on them." When a sensitive issue arises, he asks questions to help people process their feelings and thoughts about that issue, while preventing speakers from being attacked by others in the group. The facilitator is the enforcer of the ground rules.

Bryan is a black man, but he doesn't think that having white skin should prevent a pastor or another key leader from initiating Erace groups. His experience has revealed three key factors that would need to be present for a any pastor to successfully lead such a process.

- First, a facilitator would have to be initiating changes in the church that would cause the minority group to recognize that the church is serious about the vision. Specifically, the staff and other key leaders would have to include members of the minority racial or ethnic group.

- Second, a facilitator must have "street cred." Members of the minority group must view him or her as genuine and legitimate, or they will not fully enter into the process. If minority group members don't trust the facilitator, they are likely to withhold their opinions from the group.

  Bryan has already identified two couples in his church that he wants to develop into facilitators. They are volunteers, and both are biracial couples. Their experiences give them the "street cred" Bryan feels is essential to leadership of Erace groups.

- Finally, a facilitator must be willing to support worship music that ventures beyond the traditional music of the majority group.

Without such volitional steps, Bryan is sure that minority groups won't take the initiative for interracial reconciliation seriously.

THE CONTENT OF THE MEETINGS

Bryan feels that the effectiveness of Erace groups stems less from the content he has created than from the discussion it produces. The material is only a spring-board for discussion. In fact, in most meetings, not all of the material is covered. Bryan actually prefers this, as it reveals that people are engaging in the topic and the group's dialogue is taking on a life of its own. The key is to encourage spontaneous discussion, not to secure the "right" answers to questions.

Before the first meeting, Bryan gives all the participants a syllabus describing his expectations for the group, including necessary preparation. He asks members to prepare for meetings by answering questions, viewing a movie, and reading a book.

THE CRUCIAL FIRST MEETING

The first 15 minutes of the first meeting are vital to the success of the entire experience. The facilitator must establish the ground rules right away and explain that ignoring them will defeat the purpose of the group.

Because of time constraints, the facilitator must also make it clear that every issue cannot be addressed in four weeks and that no one person will be allowed to dominate the group.

But even before the first meeting, the facilitator has asked members of the group to consider their responses to a series of questions. These are not the typical questions prevalent in most small-group start-ups, the safe kind that create a warm, friendly environment. Rather, they are designed to immerse group members in the reality of the topic at hand. They intentionally cause the group's differences to rise to the surface immediately.

Week 1 Questions

1. As you were growing up, what exposure to other races did you have? Did you have meaningful relationships with people of other ethnicities or races?
2. What hurtful or helpful experiences did you have with people of other races? How did this experience shape you into the person you are today?
3. Share at least three stereotypes you have of people who are of a different race than yours.
4. Why are you here?

THE SECOND MEETING

Before the second meeting, members are asked to view the film *Crash* (2004) and be prepared to give concise answers to a series of questions. (While this film can foster intense discussion of contemporary issues concerning race, it is rated R for language, sex, and violence and is not endorsed by the publisher.) At the second meeting, they discuss the movie and their responses to these questions:

Week 2 Questions

1. With which character or characters in the movie do you most closely identify? (You have to choose at least one.) Why?
2. With which character or characters in the movie do you least identify?
3. What major lesson about race did you take away from this movie?
4. Were there any parts of the movie related to race that you felt were unrealistic?
5. Do you think racism among police and government officials is present because of the individuals who hold these positions, or do you think the system is inherently racist?
6. How much of a role does race play in our society on a day-to-day basis?

THE THIRD AND FOURTH MEETINGS

During the last two weeks of the process, members of the group discuss the book *Divided by Faith* by Michael O. Emerson and Christian Smith, which they were asked to read when they were given the syllabus.

As he introduces the discussion, Bryan reads this excerpt from the book's introduction: "This book is a story of how well-intentioned people, their values, and their institutions actually recreate racial divisions and inequalities they ostensibly oppose."

Bryan goes on to say, "In other words, even though we may sincerely say we value racial diversity and equality, the way we live may actually contribute to racial division. In your life, what are some ways in which you unintentionally contribute to racial division?" The group's answers typically concentrate on their choices of neighborhoods, schools, and friends. This discussion is carried over into the fourth meeting.

ONE-ON-ONE PEER CONNECTIONS

While participation in a four-week Erace group is a valuable experience in itself, Bryan's overarching goal is to begin interracial relationships that will last. Toward this end, he asks each group member to become a prayer partner with a group member of another race.

He's found that these partnerships work best when the partners are peers. For example, if one person is on a higher economic plane than the other, he or she may be viewed as a patron or a minister.

Bryan asks partners to call or get together for prayer once a week. They are asked to focus their prayers on racial, ethnic, and cultural issues rather than personal needs that inevitably arise.

THE DIVIDENDS

All of these efforts are beginning to change the perspectives and the hearts of the people of Fellowship Church. The most compelling outward sign of this change may be that as the congregation has grown, so has its racial diversity. In a church that started as primarily white, 30 percent of the worshippers are now black.

In addition, many of the members of this church are choosing to enter into the vision of reconciliation in concrete ways. For instance, one couple has modified their upper middle-class lifestyle by selling their home and moving into a low-income neighborhood. They want to do more than send money to the poor or say that they believe in building relationships across racial lines. They have actually stepped over racial lines and entered into the lives of their black neighbors. Rachelle Picardo and Pete Nelson lead a tutoring center for the children of Sudanese refugees who have settled in Memphis. Three nights a week, more than 100 Sudanese children get help with their homework from volunteers at the center.

> **"RACIAL AND ETHNIC HOSTILITY IS THE FOREMOST SOCIAL PROBLEM FACING OUR WORLD TODAY."**
> — BILLY GRAHAM

Bryan also asks members of his staff to make lifestyle changes that will show that they're walking the talk of racial reconciliation. He asks each staff member to befriend a peer of another race. He tells the white staff members, "You guys have a lot more power to address this goal than I do."

LESSONS LEARNED

Since beginning Erace groups, Bryan has learned a great deal about every aspect of the effort. For example, he feels that *Divided by Faith* addresses the heart of the issues that prevent churches from contributing significantly to racial reconciliation, but he also knows that the book may be too academic for some people. He is exploring other books that would lead to fruitful discussion.

> "WE MUST LEARN TO LIVE TOGETHER AS BROTHERS OR PERISH TOGETHER AS FOOLS."
> —MARTIN LUTHER KING JR.

In addition, he is considering lengthening the experience to six weeks. Because there is so much weighty material to process, he wonders if the groups can really make meaningful progress in only four weeks.

RIPPLE EFFECTS

Because people are changing as a result of their experiences in Erace groups, Bryan hopes to eventually invite everyone in the church to participate in these groups.

He wants the congregation to replicate the radical choices of people like Joey and Amy Bland. Joey and his family are quite athletic. They are taking what they love doing as a family and applying it to the vision of the church by starting a sports league in a poor black neighborhood.

As people become honest with themselves and others about their perceptions of other races, their misconceptions, stereotypes, and judgments unravel. Erace groups spark spiritual and emotional changes that cause people to make radical lifestyle changes. And that is just what is needed to build true community within the church.

CHAPTER THREE
IMPLEMENTATION

ONE STEP AT A TIME

According to Bryan, initiating an Erace group in your church will not require a great deal of preparation or training. A simple reproducible process includes four steps:

1. **Make sure leadership shares your vision.** If key leaders don't wholeheartedly embrace the need for racial reconciliation, this will be a pointless exercise. If they do share this vision, be sure to fully explain the purpose and design of Erace groups to them.

2. **Craft a list of potential pilot group members.** Don't publicly announce the Erace group strategy. Simply experiment with a couple of pilot groups, and correct any missteps before making this a key strategy of the church.

3. **Make sure the senior pastor facilitates the pilot groups.** At the very least, the senior pastor should co-facilitate these groups. Racial reconciliation must be modeled from the top down.

4. **Recruit and develop future facilitators.** Ideally, these people will have participated in the early pilot groups. Make sure they are passionate about racial reconciliation; then train them in the art of facilitating an Erace group.

FINAL THOUGHTS ABOUT...THE LONG HAUL

Bryan says that if there is anything he's learned about racial reconciliation and building community in the church, it can be summarized by the words *long haul*. He confesses that he gets frustrated by the slow nature of this kind of change, with how long and how much work it takes to address the deeply-rooted issues that have led to racial division.

Then he remembers his great-great-grandfather, Peter Loritts, who was a slave and a man of prayer. Recently, as Bryan sat in a hotel room that his ancestor would never have dreamed of being allowed to enter, Bryan realized that he is the living realization of Peter's prayers.

The work of racial reconciliation is not quick. Bryan hopes that the work he does today will create a better church and a better city for his children and their children. In order to keep at it, he has learned to view all of his efforts from the perspective of the long haul.

"AFTER THIS I LOOKED AND THERE BEFORE ME WAS A GREAT MULTITUDE THAT NO ONE COULD COUNT, FROM EVERY NATION, TRIBE, PEOPLE AND LANGUAGE, STANDING BEFORE THE THRONE AND IN FRONT OF THE LAMB." —REVELATION 7:9

CHAPTER FOUR

BUILD COMMUNITY AT
ANNUAL MEETINGS

This church has transformed its annual meeting from a boring, sparsely attended recitation of facts and figures into a community-building event that packs the house.

☑ WORKS FOR CHURCHES OF ANY SIZE

☑ TRANSFORMS A DRY BUSINESS MEETING INTO
A TIME OF ENCOURAGEMENT

☑ REQUIRES SUBSTANTIAL VOLUNTEER INVOLVEMENT AND PREPARATION

CAN THIS REALLY BE AN ANNUAL MEETING?

There was a time you had to guess when the annual meeting was underway at First United Methodist Church in Loveland, Colorado.

Ten cars dotted the parking lot. A monotone droned through open windows. And, if you peeked inside, absolutely nobody was smiling. Was it the annual meeting—or a funeral? The only way to know for certain was to see if people carried out a coffin or a stack of meeting notes.

Now the annual meeting is a standing-room-only affair. Elegantly dressed attendees come early to claim aisle seats. Cameras flash and video cameras roll as limousines glide up to the end of a plush red carpet. Dignitaries wave their way past the paparazzi who elbow each other aside to get a photo or beg for an interview.

Once inside, a smiling, tuxedoed emcee introduces presenters who announce nominated ministries for awards. Film clips appear on the screen. Live music punctuates the program, and applause thunders as winners take the stage to give their acceptance speeches.

You'd think they were at the Academy Awards...and in a way, they are.

NOW, BROADCAST LIVE FROM YOUR CHURCH...

"When it comes to our annual meeting, we've definitely had a paradigm shift," says First United Methodist's Pastor, Olon M. Lindemood. "We've gone from a meeting attended by one denominational executive and 12 grumpy people to an event that nearly blows the doors off."

But attendance isn't all that's changed.

"Our focus has shifted, too," Olon says. "Now instead of reciting statistics, we celebrate a year of ministry. And that's a lot more fun."

Adopting the Academy Awards format gave First United Methodist a chance to build excitement for a meeting that's actually a legal necessity. If your church is incorporated as a nonprofit, it's likely you, too, are obligated to hold an annual meeting—which is precisely how most churches approach their meeting: as an unwelcome duty rather than an opportunity to build community.

Letting annual meetings drift by year after year as poorly attended organizational autopsies is a missed opportunity. Instead, redeem your meeting by doing what First United Methodist has done: Transform it into an upbeat celebration of what God has done in and through your community of faith.

You'll bless a lot of people in the process.

AND NOMINATED FOR THIS YEAR'S LIFETIME ACHIEVEMENT AWARD IN MINISTRY...

One award that's always presented is a Lifetime Achievement Award. In some ways it's one of the most prestigious awards, because it's less about the previous 12 months than about the work of a lifetime.

At First United Methodist, the award has been presented to, among others, the wives of pastors, and at one particularly touching ceremony, it was given to a woman who was 90 years old and in a wheelchair.

"When the presenter opened the envelope and read her name, people stood and cheered," says Olon, who's still gets emotional talking about the event. "She was in tears. *We* were in tears. We were able to celebrate her long years of faithfulness and give witness to her life."

CHAPTER FOUR
IMPLEMENTATION

HOW TO TURN YOUR ANNUAL MEETING INTO AN ACADEMY AWARDS AFFAIR

First, keep in mind this is a *staged* event—while you could do the event without sweating details like a red carpet and envelopes for your presenters to open, it's precisely those details that make the event special.

Pulling off the event at the level experienced at First United Methodist will require you to build a team that includes people who are familiar with contemporary films and who excel in video production, sound, and computers.

In short, you need to involve your high school youth group. *Big* time.

"It's important that the production values are high," Olon asserts. "Something always goes wrong technically, but that's also true of actual awards shows. The goal is to minimize glitches and have everything go smoothly."

And, as every show producer has learned, "smooth" equals "plenty of planning." Your team will spend weeks brainstorming, filming, editing, and polishing the program until it shines like a new dime. The results will be nothing short of spectacular—and worth every minute invested.

CAST AND CREW CONSIDERATIONS

First United has discovered that the following roles are essential to pulling off a top-flight program:

Videographer—prepares the film clips that are screened during the program and tapes and edits the dress rehearsal. (More on this later.)

Roaming Camera Person—works with the videographer to provide live interviews.

Soundboard Operator—runs music sound effects before, during, and after the show. He or she drops in musical flourishes as winners walk to the stage and after their acceptance speeches.

Orchestra Conductor—stands where he or she can "direct" an offstage orchestra (the flourishes provided by the soundboard operator).

Emcee—hosts the show and introduces presenters.

Presenters—announce nominees, open envelopes, and present awards to winners.

Ushers—greet guests, distribute copies of required business meeting documents, and escort guests to seats.

Paparazzi—Armed with flash cameras, this crowd lines the red carpet to take photos (or simply set off flashes) and beg for autographs and interviews.

Spotlight Operator—operates, well, the spotlight.

Plus, of course, you'll need guests and nominees, as well as musical performers. Here are a dozen tips for rounding up the people you need, and creating an annual meeting worthy of Hollywood.

STEPS TO TAKE

1. **Determine the categories of ministry you wish to honor.** First United Methodist limits itself to nine categories per show—and the categories aren't always the same from year to year. It all depends on what the congregation wants to celebrate from the previous year's ministry.

> **THE AWARDS PROGRAM IS A WONDERFUL CHANCE TO HONOR PEOPLE WHO AREN'T USUALLY IN THE SPOTLIGHT.**
> —SANDI DILLON

Sandi Dillon, First United Methodist's student pastor and children's director, scripted the last program. "We started by getting a group of church leaders together to discuss what happened during the past year," she says. "We decided what to celebrate and who was behind the scenes making it happen. And we tried to hit all the major areas of ministry in our categories."

It is equally important to keep in mind who's been nominated for an award in the past. "We want to be sure we don't keep nominating the same people again and again," Sandi says.

Following are categories First United Methodist has used the past few years. Remember that there are too many to use in any one year, so pick and choose those that highlight significant ministry efforts in your church. Better yet—use this list as a launching pad to brainstorm your *own* categories!

Best Performance in a Caring Ministry—Include your counseling team, home-care ministry, or any other group of people who quietly serve others.

Best Performance in Outreach Ministry—Who's reaching out to the community? Celebrate them here!

Best New Worship Experience—Whether it was a flop or a hit, here's the chance to celebrate a new worship service, event, or change in your worship style.

> **THE 'ROAD TRIP' CATEGORY IS A GREAT PLACE TO SHOW EXCERPTS OF HOW MISSION FUNDS WERE USED.**
> —OLON M. LINDEMOOD

Best Road Trip—Include short-term mission trips, youth retreats, or any other trip that fired up the church bus. For example, you could reward a team that worked nonstop for four days at a hurricane-relief site.

Best Disappearing Act—Be careful with this category. If church leaders have resigned because they cycled out of leadership or relocated to another part of the country, honor them here. If a leader left for any other reason, this probably isn't the best place to mention it.

Best Use of Media Technology—Remember the youth group that pulled together all the video for your awards ceremony? Give 'em a hand!

Best Performance in a Welcoming Ministry—Consider your ushers, greeters, and people who staff the church information booth on Sunday mornings. If they communicate a warm welcome to visitors, they're eligible for a nomination in this category.

Best Event Promotion—Someone has to get the word out about the great stuff your church is doing. Who are they—and how have they been successful this past year? Tell your congregation with a nomination.

Best Fellowship Opportunity—Potlucks, church picnics, revivals—whatever gets your folks together and connecting counts here.

Best Performance as a Camp or Retreat Director—This is a wonderful way to honor the survivors of your middle school lock-in.

Best Set Design—If your VBS director and his or her team did a spectacular job decorating your church, acknowledge their efforts with this nomination.

Best Musical Score—Honor a worship leader or an entire choir. In addition to letting them perform throughout your awards ceremony, you can single them out for affirmation.

Best Achievement in Sound Technology—Who runs your soundboard? Who handles the behind-the-scenes headaches at your Christmas musical? Who put together the sound for this awards ceremony? All are potential nominees.

Best Small-Group Experience—Whether it's a church-based or home-study small-group experience, it may rate a mention here.

Best Performance While Working With Small Children—Sunday school, MOPS, and midweek workers can all take turns sharing the spotlight in this category.

2. **Be strategic in your selection of nominees and volunteers.** Picture this: You've pulled together a complete awards program with all the trimmings. Your emcee takes the stage in a flurry of fanfare and camera flashes and looks out at an audience of...six.

Ouch.

How can you be sure that you'll have a full house? that there's enthusiasm for a meeting that has, for years, been endured with a yawn?

Olon calls his strategy for guaranteeing a crowd "intentional recruitment," and it's an approach worthy of your consideration. "Keep in mind that you can nominate *groups* of people," says Olon. "We do that for several reasons.

"First, it reflects the true nature of most ministries. Most effective programs are a team effort, and we want to acknowledge and celebrate that.

"And nothing assures people's presence more than receiving a letter notifying them that they've been nominated for an award."

Notification letters don't specify which award a person has been nominated for, and, again, that's strategic. "It keeps people interested throughout the program," Sandi says.

3. **Use a scriptwriter—but expect presenters to ad lib.** It's a truth that's been proved again and again: When handed a microphone people speak longer than their allotted time. Since there may be upward of 15 people making presentations at your annual meeting, you can assume that a one-hour program will time out at about 90 minutes. If you plan for 90 minutes and warn all presenters to stick to their scripts, you'll be on track for a two-hour program.

Since the time overrun is inevitable, plan for it, and don't be stressed when it happens.

4. **Film nominees as they do ministry.** As each award category is introduced, the presenter will call out the nominees—and each nominee will be shown on the screen.

Some nominees will be bogus—film characters whose clips can easily (and legally) be lifted from contemporary or classic films. But when you're mentioning your own people, you need something to show. So during the weeks leading up to the program, collect footage of each nominee in action. Plan ahead to make sure it happens. (Every nominee will be a winner, but we'll tell you more about that later.)

5. **Carefully prescreen film clips.** Asking your youth group or a film buff in your church to select scenes from appropriate movies doesn't mean you'll get what you want. Prescreen each clip to be sure language and dress are appropriate. Also, check to ensure that the license your church has to show film clips covers the studios selected by your youth group.

> **Tip**
>
> *In general, federal copyright laws do not allow you to use videos or DVDs (even ones you own) for any purpose other than home viewing. Though some exceptions allow for the use of short segments of copyrighted material for educational purposes, it's best to be on the safe side. Your church can obtain a license from Christian Video Licensing for a small fee. Just visit www.cvli.org or call 1-888-771-2854 for more information. When using a movie that is not covered by the license, we recommend directly contacting the movie studio to seek permission to use the clip.*

To save you time, the following are some movies First United Methodist has used to highlight selected award categories. Precisely *which* few minutes you pull from each film depends on the sensibilities of your audience and the elements of the ministry you wish to spotlight. (And, as you might suspect, the mention of a movie in this list doesn't imply any endorsement of the film as a whole.)

Best Performance in a Caring Ministry: Louise Fletcher as Nurse Ratched in *One Flew Over the Cuckoo's Nest,* Angelica Huston as the wicked stepmother in *Ever After: a Cinderella Story,* Kathy Bates as Annie Wilkes in *Misery*

Best New Worship Experience: *Sister Act, My Big Fat Greek Wedding*

Best Road Trip: *The Polar Express*

Best Performance in a Welcoming Ministry: *Matilda, Lemony Snicket's A Series of Unfortunate Events, The Pacifier*

Best Event Promotion: Geoffrey Rush as Philip Henslowe in *Shakespeare in Love,* Tom Hanks as Mr. White in *That Thing You Do!*

Best Performance as a Camp or Retreat Director: Nancy Kulp as Miss Grunecker in *The Parent Trap* (1961), Jon Voight as Mr. Sir in *Holes*

Best Set Design: *The Terminal, Harry Potter and the Prisoner of Azkaban*

Best Achievement in Sound Technology: *Singin' in the Rain, Ocean's Eleven, Enemy of the State*

Best Actor: Vivien Leigh as Scarlett O'Hara in *Gone with the Wind*

Best Small-Group Experience: *Divine Secrets of the Ya-Ya Sisterhood, Peter Pan, Anger Management*

Best Performance While Working With Small Children: Bonnie Hunt and Steve Martin as the Bakers in *Cheaper by the Dozen,* Eddie Murphy as Charlie Hinton in *Daddy Day Care,* Jan Hook as Miss Leavey in *Simon Birch*

Save time! Hundreds of prescreened video clips are reviewed in several books from Group Publishing: Movie Clips for Kids, Movie Clips for Kids—The Sequel, Group's Blockbuster Movie Illustrations, Group's Blockbuster Movie Illustrations—The Sequel, *and* Group's Blockbuster Movie Illustrations—The Return *give you not only descriptions of clips but also precise locations so you can find them quickly on a video or DVD.*

---

6. **Dress up.** Communicate in invitations and announcements that this is a formal affair so attendees should come in formal attire. Don't enforce the dress code, but set the tone by having key staffers wear suits and evening dresses.

Olon rents a tuxedo for the event, and one year a denominational executive was whisked up to the door in a 1957 Rolls-Royce. "We have live video feeds of key arrivals shown on the screen inside," says Olon. "It's tightly timed and looks great."

7. **Hold a dress rehearsal—and film it.** A run-through will help your timing and allow your film team to film and edit "red carpet interviews" before your event. The completed clips can simply be dropped in during your event rather than done live.

8. **Make everyone a winner.** Here's a secret: If three Hollywood actors and one usher team from First United Methodist are all nominated for "Best Performance in a Welcoming Role Ministry," the smart money is on the ushers taking home a trophy.

    That's right, the awards are *fixed*. Shh—don't tell the Academy!

    And if three *different* usher teams are nominated, the judges will be unable to decide, so it'll be a three-way tie that makes all the teams winners.

    Your goal: to celebrate those doing ministry. So don't let any nominated person or team lose.

9. **Replace the Oscar with your own award.** It's doubtful your budget will stretch far enough to allow you to hand out 8.5 pound, 24-karat gold-plated statuettes like the actual Academy Award of Merit statues proudly carried by movie stars.

    Still, your presenters have to hand *something* to the winners of your awards.

    You can visit your local party store and, for just a few dollars, have all the gold-tone plastic statuettes you need. They'll be smaller than actual Oscars, but then again—they're actually affordable.

    Or you *could* do what a creative nonprofit did to create awards that ended up on the kitchen table instead of the fireplace mantle. The awards team bought a bunch of Aunt Jemima syrup bottles—each of which is shaped like a woman. After painting the plastic bottles gold, the bottles made impressive statuettes, and their contents were delicious!

10. **Include live music.** At First United Methodist, key music groups (the choir, the worship band, the praise team, and so on) are asked to perform Broadway show tunes. It's a crowd-pleaser and fun for the groups to perform. Performances are peppered throughout the event, and each is introduced with "And now, a live performance from one of our nominees for Best Musical Score…"

11. **Take care of business, too.** Your annual meeting has a prescribed agenda to address, and at First United Methodist that's done during a keynote address from the "academy representative."

"We distribute the materials and take votes on pastoral compensation and other items fairly quickly," says Olon, who points out that the Academy Awards format is not geared for problem solving or conflict resolution. "If there's a significant push-back about something in the agenda, it requires a separate format," Olon says.

If your agenda includes something likely to prompt an emotional debate, resolve those issues *before* your meeting. The event is designed for celebration, not heated discussions.

> **"OUR DENOMINATIONAL EXECUTIVE PRESENTS THE BUSINESS MATTERS; THIS TENDS TO MOVE THEM ALONG QUICKLY."**
> —OLON M. LINDEMOOD

"During our business section we also make room for sacred moments," Olon says. "On screen we silently scroll through the names of people who've died during the past year. And we celebrate lists of people we've baptized and who've joined our church fellowship."

12. **Consider hosting an after-party.** Serve hors d'oeuvres and sparkling cider. Snap plenty of pictures of participants talking together. Set up an interview station where your media folks can film award winners talking about how they felt being honored. People have dressed up for a fun evening; extending it with a party is another community-building opportunity.

"Time feels suspended during the event because it's so much fun," says Olon. "Our last awards ceremony lasted two and a half hours, and then people stayed for the party."

FINAL THOUGHTS ABOUT...MAKING THIS TRANSITION

Business meetings are known as much for creating dissent as they are for building unity—maybe even more so. Perhaps that's why they're such a powerful opportunity to promote community!

You can expect jaws to drop the first year you attempt to transform an annual meeting from a business forum into a time of celebration. Some people will think you're attempting to manipulate a business decision. Others will be concerned that there's not sufficient gravity surrounding a vote about whether to re-stripe the parking lot. Still others will simply be confused, convinced they've walked into the wrong meeting.

Relax. You're shifting a paradigm, and that always take a bit of time.

But the second year? Expect a standing-room-only crowd—and for the meeting to be a blessing to everyone in attendance.

And speaking of attendees, be sure there aren't any unhappy lawyers among them. The "Academy Awards" is a registered trademark of the Academy of Motion Picture Arts and Sciences Academy Foundation (8949 Wilshire Boulevard, Beverly Hills, CA, 90211; [310] 247-3000). Give credit where credit is due, carefully acknowledging the foundation in any and all printed materials.

"IF ONE PART [OF THE BODY OF CHRIST]
IS HONORED, EVERY PART REJOICES WITH IT."
—1 CORINTHIANS 12:26

BUILD COMMUNITY DURING THE 12 DAYS OF CHRISTMAS

Members of this church celebrate the 12 days of Christmas by giving gifts anonymously.

- ☑ WORKS FOR CHURCHES OF ANY SIZE
- ☑ BUILDS INTERGENERATIONAL COMMUNITY
- ☑ REQUIRES MINIMAL VOLUNTEER MANAGEMENT
- ☑ IS FUN FOR FAMILIES
- ☑ SEASONAL

A MYSTERY

It's dark, nearly midnight.

A shadow darts across the frost-crusted lawn of a suburban home. It pauses; then it inches closer to the front door.

Inside, a television announces that a cold front moving in from the Rockies might ice New Year's Eve streets, and police are warning partiers to avoid drinking and driving.

No one in the house hears footsteps creeping up the front steps. No one sees gloved hands carefully place a box just to the right of the front door. No one in the house watches as the shadowed figure turns and Pastor Brad sprints toward...

Wait a minute...*Pastor Brad?*

That's the *pastor* jumping into the passenger seat of an idling getaway car? And that's the pastor's *wife* slipping the car into gear and quietly driving through the streets of this sleeping neighborhood?

Since when have pastors and their spouses made midnight raids on parishioners?

WELCOME TO THE 12 DAYS OF CHRISTMAS

For Brad and Amy Gilliland, the 12 days of Christmas are more than the two weeks between Christmas and Epiphany or the name of a Christmas carol.

Those days are also an opportunity for hit-and-run affirmations, some of which are delivered under cover of darkness. The idea is to choose a family and deliver gifts for 12 days in a row—without getting caught.

"The first time we participated we were on the receiving end of the Christmas presents," says Brad. "It wasn't until later we decided to deliver gifts, too."

It started when Brad and Amy were newly called to pastor a church. They were just getting to know people in the community when Christmas rolled around. Like most young married couples far from home at the holidays, they were more than a little lonely. They were also more than a little surprised when a package appeared on their doorstep. "The gift wasn't elaborate," remembers

Brad. "It was a log for a Christmas fire." What made the gift more than just an oversized stick was the note that was attached to it:

"On the first day of Christmas,
My new friends gave to me
A log to warm our Christmas company."

That was it: a log, a poem, and a mystery.

The next night a second gift appeared—this time two mugs and a new poem:

"On the second day of Christmas,
My new friends gave to me
Two mugs and some chamomile tea."

"The notes we received weren't signed," says Brad. "The gifts were completely anonymous."

The gift-giving continued for 12 days, and the gifts were always accompanied by a personalized stanza modeled after the familiar 16th-century Christmas carol "The Twelve Days of Christmas."

Each night a gift and poem appeared, but who were the nocturnal gift-givers? Amy decided to catch them in the act. "I'd stand at the window in the dark, waiting," she remembers. "But they were good—I never spotted them."

What flushed out their benefactors was a request from the pulpit that the gift-givers join the Gillilands for breakfast—a request that was honored.

"Those 12 days had a real impact on us," remembers Brad. "To think that someone worked so hard to give us gifts and write poems—that was special. We felt loved."

So the Gillilands decided to pass along the blessing by becoming gift-givers, too. They chose a family, wrote poems, collected gifts, and plotted how to deliver the gifts without getting caught.

WHY PASTORS AREN'T RECRUITED AS INTERNATIONAL SPIES

"It was pretty much a disaster, as far as staying anonymous goes," laughs Amy. "Brad was found out right away."

Note to gift-givers who want to remain anonymous: Don't pull into the driveway of your target so you can drop off a gift. At least, don't do it when the family is about to get home and pull in right behind you.

"I probably could have planned that better," admits Brad.

The element of surprise makes the gift-giving more interesting because within a few days recipients are on the lookout for the donors. Like Amy, recipients are glancing out windows and peeking through curtains. The push for anonymity keeps all the folks on their toes.

And there's another benefit of staying anonymous throughout the process: It builds a sense of community.

"We didn't know whom to thank," says Amy of those 12 days when she and Brad were receiving gifts. "We figured it was someone in the church, but who?"

Because the Gillilands were unsure who was blessing them, they were thankful to everyone. They *had* to be—everyone they met at church on Sunday morning was a suspect. Anyone in church could be a person who was thinking of and caring for them.

> **STAYING UNDER-COVER DEFINITELY GETS HARDER AS THE DAYS GO BY. YOU BEGIN TO SEE THE PORCH LIGHT TURNED ON.**
> —BRAD GILLILAND

And because the Gillilands were paying extra attention to the people at their church, looking for a knowing glance or another hint to identify their benefactors, the Gillilands connected more intimately with people. They listened more carefully, made eye contact more often, and asked more questions.

They were building community.

THE HUMILITY OF RECEIVING

"I'll admit it," says Daniel, who received an anonymous gift from his church family. "I'd rather be doing the giving than the receiving. It's humbling to admit you need help—even if the need is obvious to everyone."

Daniel was handed an envelope full of cash shortly after his family's car was totaled by a hit-and-run driver. "No one was hurt, but our insurance didn't begin to replace the vehicle. Suddenly we had to buy another used car—fast—and we hadn't planned for the expense."

The gift came with a card that simply read, "A gift from some members of your family."

"At the time," says Daniel, "I hated that we needed the money. But that cash provided most of what we needed to get another car. It was a lifesaver."

It also changed how he viewed his church family.

"I know the money wasn't from just one person. Someone had gone to our church friends and told them our situation, and then collected money. There weren't any checks; it was completely anonymous. Nobody ever told me they'd contributed, and because I didn't know whom to thank, I was grateful to the entire church community. It changed how I viewed people and their faith."

Daniel received the gift 30 years ago, and he still has the card that came with the money.

"It's one of those prized possessions I'd be tempted to run back into the house to save if our home went up in flames," he says. "It's a tangible reminder that God loves me and uses his people to care for others. And it's reminded me to freely help others."

> **A GIFT FROM SOME MEMBERS OF YOUR FAMILY. NO STRINGS ATTACHED.**
> —MESSAGE IN CALLIGRAPHY ON THE FRONT OF DANIEL'S CARD

The Gillilands would agree. They've saved the poems that accompanied the gifts they received—souvenirs of an affirming experience that helped them navigate a challenging time.

CHAPTER FIVE
IMPLEMENTATION

HOW TO LAUNCH A 12 DAYS OF CHRISTMAS INITIATIVE IN YOUR CHURCH

The first thing to consider when planning a program like this is that maybe you shouldn't do it at all.

Not much of an endorsement—but consider the challenges.

"To get 12 presents and deliver them takes some time," admits Brad. "I don't know if you could do this on a large scale. It's more a small group or family thing."

But while it's not necessarily a churchwide initiative, giving 12 days of Christmas gifts is a great way to cement friendships between families or between members of an adult Sunday school class or a small group. The commitment required to see through 12 days of anything makes this a lavish display of friendship—and a memorable one.

And once you've been the recipient of 12 days of Christmas gifts, it's nearly impossible not to want to do what the Gillilands did: become gift-givers and longtime friends of people they've befriended and who have befriended them.

"What builds community isn't necessarily the gifts," Brad confirms. "It's the thought that goes into picking them and the commitment to getting the gifts to the people you want to bless."

Good point: When you invest in people, they become important to you—and that launches friendships and community. It's not only a solid emotional truth—it's a spiritual one, too. After all, God "so loved the world that he *gave* his one and only Son." God invested heavily—and as recipients of that gift we can choose to respond by giving back.

> **❝ FOR GOD SO LOVED THE WORLD THAT HE GAVE HIS ONE AND ONLY SON, THAT WHOEVER BELIEVES IN HIM SHALL NOT PERISH BUT HAVE ETERNAL LIFE. ❞**
> —JOHN 3:16

But giving *12 days'* worth of gifts to someone? If that seems like overkill, there are alternatives (more about those later). Assuming you want to dive into a full-scale 12 days of Christmas effort as a congregation or even as a family project, here are some tips from the Gillilands:

DECIDE *WHICH* 12 DAYS YOU WANT TO CELEBRATE

Christians from non-liturgical churches sometimes think the "12 days" refer to the days leading up to Christmas. In the vast majority of the Western Church, that's not the case.

Typically the 12 days begin on December 26 and end on Epiphany, January 6. If the recipients of your gifts are accustomed to celebrating the traditional period, having a "12 days" present and poem land on their doorstep on December 14 will be more baffling than a blessing.

KEEP THE ENTIRE FAMILY IN MIND

If you're giving gifts to a family, be sure that some days your gifts are most appropriate for children in the family. And while Brad and Amy have so far drawn the line at giving gifts intended for family pets, that isn't necessarily out of the question. It might be both fun and remarkably inexpensive to greet your friends with something like this:

> *On the seventh day of Christmas,*
> *(My new friends thought this up)*
> *Seven biscuits for our favorite pup!*

CONSIDER TRAVEL PLANS

The holidays are busy travel times, and you don't want your gift recipients to come home to find six presents frozen on their front steps or the homemade muffins you prepared turned into croutons.

Do your research so your friends receive a welcome gift each day.

BE SNEAKY

Ask a neighbor to deliver the box on your behalf. Deliver it during the day when people are at work. Or deliver it at night when everyone is asleep and the Neighborhood Watch is looking the other way. Leave the box with the receptionist at your friends' work site. Use the mail or a delivery service. Place the gift on the hood of the family's car, and then call (watch out for caller ID!) to notify the family the gift has been delivered. Have the package waiting at church.

Especially if you've always enjoyed James Bond movies, this is a situation in which the giver can truly enjoy the process more than the recipient!

DON'T SPEND LOTS OF MONEY

"It's truly the thought that counts," says Brad Gilliland, which means delivering 12 Christmas napkins counts as much as delivering 12 pieces of crystal stemware. Gifts don't need to be extravagant—and shouldn't be.

Brad suggests planning ahead if you're on a budget. "Most Christmas items are discounted by half or three-quarters during the week after Christmas. That's the time to buy most of your gifts. You can use them right away or keep them for the following year."

Besides, the gifts are only part of the experience.

"It's the poem that makes this so much fun," Brad says, "So personalize the poem as much as you can."

Not sure where to start when drafting poetry? Following is one alternative— use it as a launching pad for creating your own 12 days of gift-giving!

On the first day of Christmas,
My new friends gave to me
A loaf of wheat bread from the bakery.

On the second day of Christmas,
My new friends gave to me
Two pretty mittens to keep me frost-free.

On the third day of Christmas,
For children needing naps:
Three Christmas books to read on Mommy's lap.

On the fourth day of Christmas,
Look what I have found:
Four ornaments, all pretty, red, and round.

On the fifth day of Christmas,
My wondering eyes behold
Five Christmas candles to keep me from the cold.

On the sixth day of Christmas,
My new friends gave to me
A mug filled with six lovely bags of tea.

On the seventh day of Christmas,
My new friends gave to me
Seven pens and Christmas stationery.

On the eighth day of Christmas,
Eight Christmas napkins here
Remind me that my new friends hold me dear.

On the ninth day of Christmas,
I can plainly see
Nine shiny quarters to spend just on me.

On the 10th day of Christmas,
My new friends gave to me
Ten songs on a holiday CD.

On the 11th day of Christmas,
My new friends brought my way
Eleven pine boughs for this special day.

On the 12th day of Christmas,
My new friends must be near:
A dozen doughnuts fuel my Christmas cheer!

FINAL THOUGHTS ABOUT...AN ALTERNATIVE

If 12 days of gift-giving seems about nine days too long, here's a plan for scaling back the complexity and still having fun.

Within your small group or Sunday school class, invite people to join in an anonymous gift exchange. Participants receive the name of another person who signed up and then buy that person inexpensive gifts. If possible arrange the pairings so participants receive the names of people they don't know already—discovering what another person likes or enjoys is part of the community-building process.

Agree on both a number of gifts to be exchanged (three works well) and dates on which those gifts will be exchanged anonymously. For example, perhaps an adult Sunday school class would pick three Sundays between Thanksgiving and Epiphany on which to bring wrapped presents to a classroom at church. At the end of class, the gifts would be distributed to recipients so they can be opened in a group setting.

An encouragement: Keep the pairing of recipients the same throughout the gift exchange. It prompts deeper discovery when Jack has to find out enough about Ralph to provide three presents instead of just one. For instance, Jack may already know Ralph likes coffee—he shows up to class with a cup each Sunday. But since Jack can't give Ralph three coffee mugs, Jack needs to ask around until he discovers Ralph's also a woodworker (who can always use more nails) and he enjoys model railroads.

It's that investment in gleaning information that builds community—not the gifts themselves.

"If you do a gift exchange, it's important that givers and receivers eventually meet and get to know each other," says Brad. "That's what launches the friendships."

Finally, a caution: It's awkward if only 14 of the 25 members of an adult Sunday school class participate. Keeping the spending limit low—even $5 to $10, total, for three gifts—can make it affordable for everyone.

Remember, the point isn't in getting—or even giving—gifts. The point is to focus attention on others and to invest in knowing and encouraging those people.

That's when we build memories and bonds that become community.

"DO NOT LET YOUR LEFT HAND KNOW WHAT YOUR RIGHT HAND IS DOING, SO THAT YOUR GIVING MAY BE IN SECRET. THEN YOUR FATHER, WHO SEES WHAT IS DONE IN SECRET, WILL REWARD YOU."
—MATTHEW 6:3-4

BUILD COMMUNITY AMONG CHILDREN AND ADULTS

This church connects children with caring adults who pray for them throughout the year.

- ☑ WORKS FOR CHURCHES OF ANY SIZE
- ☑ FOSTERS INTERGENERATIONAL MINISTRY
- ☑ BUILDS CHILDREN'S MINISTRY
- ☑ REQUIRES SOME VOLUNTEER MANAGEMENT

CHAPTER SIX

PRAYING FOR CHILDREN

Dave Kirkham knew that praying for his children was important, and he'd long made it a daily habit. But sitting in a worship service one Sunday at New Beginnings Free Methodist Church near Oneida, New York, it struck him that praying for *other* people's children might be a good idea, too. And if he was willing to do it, so might other adults in his congregation.

In fact, Dave couldn't think of a good reason why *all* of the children in the church shouldn't have adults other than their parents praying for them daily—people willing to form relationships with the children and pray specifically for things that mattered to each individual child.

What each child needed, Dave felt, was a prayer warrior. A prayer partner. A prayer pair. Or even better—a prayer *bear.*

WELCOME TO PRAYER BEAR CENTRAL

First, a word about the name.

"Children often have teddy bears for comfort, support, and love," Dave says. "I figured the same could be said for their Prayer Bears."

Fine...but *Prayer Bears?*

Dave, New Beginnings' children's pastor, answers with a smile, "Hey—it rhymes. And it works."

At New Beginnings it works so well that nearly 200 children are involved in the program. That's 200 children who each have an adult in the congregation praying for them daily and checking in weekly to see if they have prayer requests.

"It's awesome," says Jeanette Holdridge, who should know. She has three children in the program and is a Prayer Bear herself. "It's *incredibly* powerful."

KEEPING IT SIMPLE

"The biggest challenge is to keep the program simple," says Dave, who has pared the idea down to the basics. "We have only two rules for the adults who sign up to pray for children.

"First, they have to take the program seriously. When they commit to praying daily for the child they choose, that's exactly what the commitment means. Daily prayer. Daily as in *every* day.

"Second, Prayer Bears can't choose their own kids or grandkids. They should be praying for those kids already. We want them to pick children they wouldn't normally pray for.

"That's it. The rest is details."

Of course, it's those details that make the program manageable and that build intergenerational community within New Beginnings. And it's those details that allow the program to safely connect adults with children.

"We live in a dangerous world," Dave says. "Parents want to know who has information about their children and which adults their children are trusting. That's why we never include a child in the program unless his or her parent says its OK."

Parents must approve a request to enter their child's name and other information in a database and to take a photo of the child that will be given to another adult in the congregation.

Prayer Bears each receive a child's photo, name, and several pieces of information that make it easier to initiate a relationship: the child's date of birth, favorite color, favorite foods, and a short list of hobbies or favorite sports.

Dave keeps photos in a three-ring binder, and he never lets the binder out of his sight throughout the Prayer Bear registration process. Adults who wish to serve as Prayer Bears can't simply grab a child's picture and information and then go; they need to provide identification and contact information and be linked to a specific child.

To complete the loop, Dave then tells parents which adults will be their children's Prayer Bears. That way everyone has the same information, and no relationships are anonymous.

An additional safeguard is Dave's expectation that Prayer Bears build a relationship with children *and* their parents. Parents need to control when and where Prayer Bears communicate with their children; informed parents are the best possible safeguards against inappropriate behavior or predators.

> **SO FAR OUR PROGRAM HAS BEEN FOR CHILDREN UP TO SIXTH GRADE. BUT NEXT YEAR WE'RE EXPANDING TO INCLUDE TEENAGERS.**
> —DAVE KIRKHAM

WHAT EXACTLY DO PRAYER BEARS DO?

While Dave doesn't hand out official 50-page Prayer Bear manuals, he does share several expectations with adults serving in the role:

First and foremost, they pray. "Sometimes people don't understand how important prayer is," says Jeanette. "My children who have Prayer Bears ask for specific prayer support. Their requests are as simple as doing well on a test or as complex as dealing with peer pressure. My daughters are very encouraged knowing that adult friends are praying for them."

Dave urges Prayer Bears to tape the child's photo to the refrigerator door or another prominent place so that it will serve as a prayer prompt. "It's all about praying for the children," he says. "Great things happen when children are lifted up in prayer."

By far the greatest benefit Dave has seen is the relationships formed between Prayer Bears and their adopted kids. "At church you see grown-ups making connections with kids. Maybe it's a high five or a quick hug or a couple of words exchanged in a hallway. It's all good—and it all makes the kids feel special and loved."

They initiate relationships. "We tell Prayer Bears to reach out to form a relationship with the family," Dave says. "Prayer Bears pick up the phone and call parents so everyone connects early in the process. Parents then have the chance to ask questions and feel comfortable with this new adult who'll be talking with their kids.

"Then there's initiating the relationship with the child, but first things first. Parents come first."

One benefit of adults getting to know each other is the sense of community it engenders. Parents love talking about their children; to find listening, interested ears is a blessing...and often the launching pad for an ongoing relationship.

They look for the children at church. Jeanette looks for the children for whom she's praying each Sunday at church. "Even brief one-on-one contact is encouraging," she says. "A quick hug, a high five, a 'hello'—I ask if there's anything new going on or if there's anything I can pray about. Sometimes there is, and sometimes there isn't, but I always check. I'm sending the message 'I'm praying for you; I'm out here; I'm in your corner.' "

Thanks to technology Jeanette has found additional contact points. "My Prayer Bear kids and I have started communicating daily by e-mail. They're now asking me if there's anything going on in my life about which *I* want prayer. How cool is *that?*"

They acknowledge special occasions. Small gifts at Christmas or on birthdays, a Valentine's card and box of chocolates—all are appropriate reminders that Prayer Bears are thinking of children. And as Prayer Bears learn more about their kids, other special occasions that might prompt celebration or sympathy become obvious.

Prayer Bears are perfect people to send congratulations cards to honor the passing of an especially challenging exam or to applaud winning an award or basketball game. A "thinking of you" e-card can provide a bright spot during a difficult transition from elementary to middle school. And Prayer Bears are perfect people to drop by with a hug when a pet or grandparent dies.

They serve when the opportunity arises.

When Emily, one of Jeanette's daughters, was in the hospital for an extended stay, her Prayer Bear did more than just pray.

"Emily's Prayer Bear made daily contact with Emily and then offered to serve as the bridge between our family and the larger church family who wanted to know how Emily was doing."

The Prayer Bear fielded phone calls and provided daily updates and reports. Her efforts helped Jeanette's family stay focused on Emily and allowed church friends to pray more effectively for Emily.

"I'm a big believer in keeping things simple," says Dave. "The Prayer Bear program boils down to this: We're asking caring adults to build relationships with children and to pray for those kids. To ask if there are any special prayer requests. To check in with parents. And then to pray daily. That's it."

CHAPTER SIX
IMPLEMENTATION

NUTS AND BOLTS

If you're considering launching a similar program at your church, here are seven tips that might help.

KEEP FIRST THINGS FIRST

The Prayer Bear program isn't about evangelism. It's not designed to be a recruiting tool for your children's ministry—though it may certainly boost the program's visibility and result in new volunteers. Rather, the program exists to pair each child in your church with a concerned adult who will pray for that child.

Prayer is the point, and a desire to pray effectively drives the relationships between Prayer Bears and the families they serve. From that simple idea, relationships are formed, community is cemented, and generations are connected.

But prayer is the point.

START WITH PARENTS

Nothing fires off warning flares faster for parents than hearing their children say, "Yeah, someone came to our Sunday school class and wrote down our favorite stuff. Then he took our pictures."

Let parents know what's coming and that participation is optional.

"I promote the program from the pulpit," Dave says. "I promote it as a way for the entire congregation to be involved in children's ministry. I mean, not everyone can teach a lesson or lead music, but everyone *can* pray for a child." That pulpit appearance reassures parents that the Prayer Bear program is approved by church leadership.

Dave hasn't yet had a parent choose not to let his or her child be involved, but he always checks. Every year. Regarding each child.

"Parents don't want surprises about something like this," he says.

RELAUNCH THE PROGRAM EVERY YEAR

Kids come; kids go. Kids move away. Their families switch churches. There are a dozen reasons to update your database annually and get parents' permission to include their children in the program.

Of course, you may find that a child enters your church the week after you've wound up your annual launch. What happens then?

"If that child's parents hear about the program and want to involve their child, our answer is 'of course.' We'll quietly find a Prayer Bear who is willing to pray for another child."

LEAVE NO CHILD BEHIND

It happens: You'll have a hundred photos of children available for "adoption," and after a week a handful of photos remain....and remain...and are *still* there two weeks later.

What do you tell those children? That nobody cares enough about them to be their Prayer Bears?

"After three weeks we children's ministry workers adopt those kids ourselves," Dave says. "We aren't going to let any child who wants a Prayer Bear go without one."

One way Dave avoids the problem is to post photos gradually over a month. "We post 50 each week over the course of a month," he explains. That way if a child isn't chosen the first week, he's in with a group of 50 fresh faces the next week. He's not sitting alone in an otherwise empty album."

Dave's policy means that children's ministry volunteers may end up with two or three children each. "But so far that's not been a problem," he says. "We're people who *like* kids."

RESPECT CONFIDENTIALITY—TO A POINT

As with any program that brings grown-ups and children together, it's critical that trust develops. That suggests confidentiality, which is fine...within reason.

Check with professionals in your area, but a rule of thumb is that maintaining confidentiality is essential unless a child threatens to hurt himself or others or the child divulges that something illegal is happening.

IT'S FIRST COME, FIRST SERVED WHEN CHOOSING KIDS

Prayer Bears can choose which children to adopt, and some want to select kids they know. Others don't care which child they're paired with; they're happy to have an opportunity to form a relationship.

"I tell volunteers that as soon as photos are available, *that's* the time to choose the kids they want," Dave says. "Some Prayer Bears choose the same children from year to year, and others pick new ones. So far it's always worked out."

KICK THE PROGRAM'S TIRES NOW AND THEN

Dave occasionally questions random kids at church about whether they're hearing from their Prayer Bears. It's a sort of quality control; Dave wants to know whether communication is frequent and positive. If children don't know who their Prayer Bears are or haven't heard from a Prayer Bear lately, Dave follows up.

FINAL THOUGHTS ABOUT...TRUST

The informality of Dave's approach might make some church leaders nervous. After all, many other organizations that pair adults and children require background checks, referrals, and screening interviews.

For good reason, according to former pastor Brian Proffit. Brian is the senior editor of Church Volunteer Central, a Web-based association that helps churches build strong, dedicated teams of volunteers. (See www.churchvolunteercentral.com for details.)

"I wish we lived in a time when we didn't need to worry about such things," says Brian, "but such worries are all too real.

"The sad truth is that predators know where the prey is easiest, and the open, trusting environment of churches is a rich hunting ground. We assume people are telling us the truth or that everybody knows everything about each other in our small town or that God will protect children in the church. As a result, we make it all too easy for those looking for access to our children.

"The Prayer Bear idea is a great way to provide loving support and adult role models for children. But just as we would be cautious in protecting other assets, we have a responsibility to be cautious in protecting these little ones."

And, Brian cautions, "many church liability insurance policies now require churches to conduct background checks on all volunteers who come into contact with children. If the church fails to do so, it may not be covered. And juries have been generous in requiring churches to make huge payments to victims.

"That's why Church Volunteer Central offers discounted background checks to our members. As a pastor, I hate that churches have been put in this position; I'm uncomfortable with background checks being part of our association at all. But it's no longer optional, and we want to help churches accomplish the checks as easily and inexpensively as possible."

Brian maintains, "This goes beyond trying to protect ourselves from legal exposure. We have a responsibility to God to be good stewards of the children he sends to us. How can we insist that two people be present when the money is counted and yet let someone we barely know be alone with our children?"

As Dave Kirkham knows, parents want to be sure that their children are being well taken care of. According to Brian, "If you can tell parents that every volunteer in your church has been through a background check, they will know you truly value their children. If you insist that they sign a permission form before their children can participate in the program, they will know that you're being careful to honor their role as parents."

Finally, Brian says, "The fact that some might use churches to prey upon children is horrible to think about, and most of us would prefer not to. It means that great ideas like the Prayer Bear program require more time and effort. But every week we hear of problems at another church that was just too trusting. Don't stop doing such great things for kids; just be conscious of the responsibility God expects shepherds to show for their sheep."

"LET THE LITTLE CHILDREN COME TO ME, AND DO NOT HINDER THEM, FOR THE KINGDOM OF GOD BELONGS TO SUCH AS THESE."
—LUKE 18:16

CHAPTER SEVEN
BUILD COMMUNITY BEFORE AND AFTER WORSHIP

A small church in Florida launches a coffee café and dozens of relationships as well.

☑ WORKS FOR CHURCHES OF ANY SIZE

☑ BUILDS INTERGENERATIONAL COMMUNITY

☑ REQUIRES GOOD VOLUNTEER MANAGEMENT

ATTRACTING A
NEW GENERATION

When Stephanie Caro was asked to pastor a new contemporary worship service in a Florida church, she jumped at the chance. "I loved the idea," she says.

Unfortunately, there were a few hurdles to clear:

- The contemporary service didn't actually exist—she'd have to start it.
- Not everyone in the congregation was likely to support changes that would make an additional worship service "contemporary."
- The average age of the current church members was pushing 80.

Stephanie knew the congregation had been in a long, steady decline. "There were no children in the congregation. None. And our sanctuary, which seats about 600, was lucky to have 60 people in it on a Sunday morning."

But church leaders weren't content to let the congregation—St. James United Methodist Church in St. Petersburg, Florida—simply fade away. In addition to serving the needs of the existing, mostly elderly church members, the leadership team wanted to provide meaningful worship experiences for 20- and 30-somethings who lived in the area but didn't attend church.

Stephanie, a 20-year career youth pastor, realized the church brought several strengths to the table. In addition to a sincere desire to grow and serve, there was the building itself.

"The space is great," she says. "Gen-Xers and Millennials like traditional church buildings like ours. They're attracted to the stained glass and the awe-inspiring sanctuary."

The problem, she realized, was that the traditional worship structure didn't feel relevant to younger adults. The challenge wasn't the content of the worship, but the style...and that meant Stephanie needed to develop an alternative worship experience that would speak to younger people.

So she organized Christ's Coffee Café.

THE POWER OF COMMUNITY

You might ask what launching an in-church coffee house has to do with starting a contemporary worship service to complement the existing traditional service.

You wouldn't be the first to pose that question. The answer lies in two things Stephanie knows are true about young adults:

1. **What's relevant to young adults is all over the map.** It may be music, information, or experiences. It may be electronic and downloadable or a moment lived in silence in the midst of nature. Relevance is in the eye of the beholder, and few demographics have a wider definition of *relevant* than young adults.

   Adding a drum set and lighting a few candles wouldn't automatically make traditional church relevant to young adults. Neither would topical studies or a more relaxed teaching style. For church to be relevant, something else had to happen: relationships.

2. **Relationships are *always* relevant.** Most young adults feel a tremendous hunger for connecting with others. They want to be with others, explore ideas with others, be in relationship with others. They're drowning in information. What they need and want is *community.*

Stephanie knew that a sense of community would attract young adults—and as they joined that community she'd have permission to speak into their lives. Belonging would come before believing.

So she set out to create a warm, welcoming place where everyone could experience a sense of belonging, a place community could form and then naturally feed into the contemporary worship experience she planned for her church. She realized that on the current cultural landscape, nothing beats a coffee house for creating a warm ambience that can lead to community.

The coffee house–worship service connection drove a few decisions for Stephanie. For instance, the coffee house couldn't be far from the worship service. In a perfect world, the relaxed sharing in the coffee house would carry on into the worship service itself. The coffee house needed to be large enough to allow people to connect and talk, yet small enough to feel intimate and inviting.

A coffee café tucked into a corner of the church sanctuary fit the bill perfectly.

"It was sort of a 'Starbucks meets Jesus' thing," Stephanie says.

THE RESULTS

Stephanie and her husband set up the coffee café with tables, chairs, sofas, and other furniture they "borrowed" from nooks and crannies of the church building, and at the same time implemented a contemporary worship service.

Within a year, the service was drawing between 75 and 85 people on any given Sunday morning.

The people attending the contemporary service aren't the same ones who were attending the original worship service. These are *new* people, and while a few Boomers and even older folks dot the contemporary worship service, most worshippers are precisely the young adults Stephanie was asked to target.

"We even have teenagers bringing their friends," she says. "That hadn't happened for a very long time at our church."

"People come early for the worship service so they can stop in the café and greet their friends. People hang out, talk, laugh, and spend time together."

Then, coffee cups in hand, they walk a few steps to where the worship service is about to begin.

HURDLES

In spite of wanting Stephanie to encourage the involvement of young people, turning a corner of the sanctuary into a coffee café didn't go down as smoothly as a double tall nonfat latte for some folks. There was grumbling—and a few upset church members.

"We have some folks who think serving coffee in church is from Satan," says Stephanie. "But at this point, we couldn't separate the worship service from the café even if we wanted to. They're parts of the same experience, parts of the same story."

It's a story that includes Scott Riley, 22, who'd grown up in the traditional church but drifted away. Scott plays bass in the contemporary worship service band, and he's a regular at the café.

"What drew me back was the chance to make connections," he says. "The café is where everyone comes together before the service to talk and interact. Now it's not about people sitting alone in pews and then taking off. They really get to know each other."

Scott is encouraged to find a sense of community at church, and he enjoys that this community isn't composed of people who are all identical, all exactly like him. "One of my favorite people ever is Janet," he says. "I always give her a hug when I see her at the café, and she's in her 80s."

RIPPLE EFFECTS

Stephanie breaks into a wide smile as she lists the benefits that have come to St. James through the coffee café.

"There have been deep enough relationships formed that people who got to know each other in the café are hanging out when they're not here," she says. "Some people are having meals together during the week and forming lasting friendships.

"On top of that, four or five small groups meet regularly. People are getting together to talk about their lives and God's Word. That's even more community and spiritual growth.

"And because some young adults have kids, our church has a children's ministry again. During the contemporary worship service, we have Kids Club, a multi-aged ministry for elementary children."

Children enjoy another innovation: Stephanie's husband, Steve Caro, manages the café, and he's reserved a corner of the café just for kids. In the Kids Café, children find small tables and chairs at which to enjoy their café snacks.

CHAPTER SEVEN
IMPLEMENTATION

HOW TO MAKE IT HAPPEN
AT YOUR CHURCH

First, don't assume that serving coffee in your sanctuary will accomplish much. Remember that Stephanie's goal wasn't to provide caffeine; it was to facilitate community.

"This may not be for everyone," she says. "Maybe there are other ways to bring about community, and that's fine. But for the young adults we wanted to involve, this is working for us."

If you *do* decide to initiate a café, here are some suggestions to keep in mind:

Start by asking if someone already knows how to do it. Steve, who manages the café, asked lots of questions. "One of our church members owned a café, and I got a lot of tips from him," says Steve. "For example, he suggested we buy coffee wholesale. I hadn't thought of that."

Who in your church has retail experience in food service? Who knows which end of an espresso machine is up? You won't need expensive equipment, but it's smart to figure out what you do—and don't—require to crank out an excellent cup of coffee.

If nobody in your congregation has this kind experience, find someone who does. Describe your plans to the manager of a local coffee house (making it clear you *aren't* competition), and get some free advice. Over a cup of coffee, of course. And you buy.

Keep it simple. It's easy to complicate a café. Do you *really* need a menu board? Matching tablecloths? To be open before and after *every* service? Twenty-seven coffee options?

What's the least complicated way you could provide a community-building space? That's the question you need to ask...and answer.

Select the location carefully. If you want a seamless flow between the worship experience and the café, locate the café where patrons will know when the worship service starts. At St. James specific songs are played when the worship service is about to begin. After a few weeks, everyone realized these signals and began wandering into the sanctuary on cue.

Proximity does count, by the way. Stephanie says, "Locate your café in the sanctuary if possible. I wouldn't put it on the altar, but I'd get as close as possible."

Establish a look and feel for the café. This can be challenging, especially if you're using a corner of a larger room. But let's face it: Most for-profit coffee houses or cafes are in reality adult clubhouses. They have grown-up snacks, grown-up furniture, and grown-ups milling around and talking. They're social clubs designed to help grown-ups feel at home.

You can accomplish this by being intentional about how you decorate your café. Take Steve's lead, and pilfer some old furniture from around the church building—chairs, tables, and couches. Arrange the furniture to encourage conversations. Make the space comfortable and inviting.

Be thoughtful about how this all plays with your church leadership, though. "Our church trustees were concerned about coffee spills on the carpet," says Steve. "They asked us to put down area rugs."

It was a small compromise—and it will be a small one for you, too.

Don't do it all yourself. Recruit expertise from the congregation, and let others help you. The whole experience will be especially powerful if as many people as possible are involved in the community you're creating.

At St. James a graphic artist who was stopping by contributed a logo for the café. Other patrons painted coffee cups on the tabletops, and still others have given advice about music. Some regulars have donated music CDs.

When people invest something of themselves in a project, it becomes more meaningful to them. Encourage people to actually implement the good ideas they'll toss your way once your café opens. Explain that the café is a work in progress and that their help is appreciated.

And be mindful that this is true whether the members of your emerging community are 26...36...or 86.

MORE SPECIFICALLY...

You can formalize the "don't do it yourself" recommendation by doing the following:

Form teams. Unless you want to be forever doomed to setting up, making coffee, taking orders, and cleaning up, form service teams to support the café.

Create a schedule and make it official. Share the work. Remember, you're also sharing the personal investment.

Keep an eye on the money. At St. James there's no charge for coffee or snacks, but a donation jar is prominently displayed. The idea isn't to maximize profits, but there is some stewardship involved.

Know what you're spending and what money is coming in. Be able to give an account for it. That's what other areas of your church's ministry do, and you should have the same financial discipline.

At St. James the monthly investment in the café, after the expenses and donations are totaled, is about $60. Given the growth prompted by the café and contemporary worship service, there's no doubt it's a good use of money. But if there was no way to track expenses, there *might* be a doubt...so Stephanie has a solid command of the financials.

One reason expenses are so low is that much of the food is donated. One patron is a baker, and she's adopted the café as her personal ministry. The biscotti she donates is a tasty addition to the menu.

Avoid an "us vs. them" mentality. Stephanie realized that if coffee were available *only* for the contemporary worship service, coffee-lovers at the more traditional worship service might feel slighted. The café is open long enough to allow attendees from both services to have access.

Remain flexible. Stephanie had no hard-and-fast formula or business plan in place before launching the café. "We've sort of made it up as we've gone along," she says, adding, "and that's probably not a bad thing."

Because the café's direction and growth have been organic, influenced by the preferences of the emerging community using it, it has stayed relevant and useful. Stephanie hesitates to put too many guidelines in cement, preferring to let the café's evolution continue. She's not certain precisely how the café will look in a year or two, but here's what she's hoping to see: lots of people talking.

"If members of our congregation are gathered, connecting and deepening their friendships, that's a success," she says. "The café will continue as long as it's helping that community form. Maybe in a few years, something else will take the café's place. If so, fine. But until then we'll keep serving coffee—and smiling as we do."

There's another reason that Christ's Coffee Café has Stephanie smiling.

"I've been in ministry more than 20 years," she says. "I'm not surprised very often. But the café's impact has surprised me, and that's cool. It's great to be excited after 20 years in ministry."

LESSONS LEARNED

Here are a few lessons that Christ's Coffee Café manager, Steve Caro, has learned the hard way:

You have to provide several flavors of excellent coffee. The days of "just gimme a cup of coffee—black" are long past. While the variety of your offerings can't compete with your local boutique coffee house, you can be sure that what you do serve is top-quality and tasty.

Offer a child-friendly cold drink, too. It doesn't really matter whether you serve orange juice, apple juice, or cider. What counts is that you have at least one coffee alternative that's acceptable to young children and non-coffee drinkers. If you don't take this step, you'll communicate that only coffee drinkers are welcome. Not exactly a community-friendly message to send.

Don't use plastic foam cups. Serve drinks in domed cups because image matters. You're aiming for "upscale," not "fishing trip."

Whipped cream matters. On at least one drink, offer whipped cream. Why? Because you can, that's why. And kids of all ages love it.

Be sure snacks are home-baked or of the same quality you'd find at a boutique coffee house. No packaged cookies or leftovers from children's ministry snack time, please.

Play edgy music. Exactly *how* edgy is up to you, but since music is one way to establish your café space as a unique gathering place, push the envelope a bit. Ask the people you're trying to attract what music attracts them.

FOUR EASY WAYS TO ADAPT THIS IDEA

Here's the truth about community: Sometimes it forms around activities. Drinking a cup of coffee is one such activity, but here's a short list of others that churches have used to successfully deepen their sense of community:

- **Play areas**—If your church has a play area or a playground, open it up between services (under supervision, of course). Parents of small children are often looking to connect with each other for support and encouragement. Where better than a playground?

- **Square dances**—Swing that partner round and round, and eventually you'll end up dancing with dozens of people. Plus, even two-left-feet dancers can handle some square dances.

- **A community garden**—Do you have some spare lawn at your church? Build a few garden beds, and invite the neighborhood to raise vegetables and flowers there. Ask several church members who live nearby to get involved by encouraging gardeners to meet one another and serving as a bridge to the church.

- **Short-term mission trips**—When well organized and appropriate, mission teams not only help others, but they also grow close in the process. Once you've hauled cement blocks with someone for eight hours, you have a common memory (and backache) that you'll never forget.

What these activities have in common is they give people an opportunity to talk—not just do an activity. It's the talking and sharing that spark relationships, not the activity.

FINAL THOUGHTS ABOUT...CHANGE

Community and caffeine—it's a potent combination!

But don't miss the even *more* potent piece of the puzzle at St. James United Methodist Church: a commitment on the part of existing church members to support change...to invite new people into the fellowship...to set aside personal preference in favor of outreach...to value community more than comfort.

If you've ever been tempted to think that senior citizens aren't willing to embrace change, visit St. James. They'll probably offer you a cup of coffee while you're there.

"A CUP OF COFFEE SHARED WITH A FRIEND
IS HAPPINESS TASTED AND TIME WELL SPENT."
—ANONYMOUS

CHAPTER EIGHT

BUILD COMMUNITY THROUGH LONG-TERM SHARE GROUPS

Small groups come, small groups go...but at this church, some groups have lasted more than 20 years.

☑ WORKS FOR CHURCHES OF ANY SIZE

☑ PROMOTES SMALL GROUPS

☑ FAMILY ORIENTED

☑ REQUIRES MINIMAL VOLUNTEER MANAGEMENT

THE BEGINNING OF
LIFELONG FRIENDSHIPS

Years ago, during a church-sponsored renewal weekend, someone suggested that church members at Applewood Baptist Church in Wheat Ridge, Colorado, get together in small groups. Roy Miller wasn't much interested in the idea—as a card-carrying introvert, Roy had about as many friends as he figured he needed. But before Roy could come up with a suitable excuse to opt out, he and his family were signed up to go to a meeting.

The good news was that some of the people in the small group were already Roy's friends. The bad news: Other people in the group weren't.

But ever the optimist, Roy decided to give it a try. If things didn't work out, he could always be too busy, have to miss meetings because of other commitments, or find another reason to fade from the group.

That was in 1972. Twenty-one years later, Roy was still a member of the group—and it had changed his life. Roy would still be in the group today if he and his wife hadn't moved away.

SMALL GROUPS AND COMMUNITY

It's no news that small groups provide fertile ground for relationships to grow and for church members to experience community. It's a rare church that hasn't launched a small-group program.

Some groups are organized around life stages or circumstances—single parents, say, or mothers of middle schoolers. Other groups are geographically based, encouraging church members who live near one another to get together. Still others are activity groups, connecting people who enjoy hiking, rock climbing, or antiquing with the hope that relationships will develop and deepen as people pursue their hobbies together.

What all those groups have in common is that usually, within a year or two, they disappear. Or, if they're still around, they're populated with mostly new people; founding members have moved on.

Are these short-term small groups helpful in building community? Yes. Do they provide connections and shared experiences that encourage relationships? Absolutely.

But what if a group stuck together for more than a year or two? What if it lasted 10 years? or 20? What if group members not only got acquainted, but became friends who walked through life together?

That would be community.

Roy wouldn't trade his 21 years in his small group for anything. "The years in our share group have been years of refreshment for us. It's been a rich, rich experience."

WHY LONG-TERM SMALL GROUPS ARE SO RARE

We live in a mobile society. Many small groups separate because the people in them move away or group members change churches. There's not much you can do to buck these societal trends.

But other small groups are actually *designed* to fold after a short time. They're formed to study through the Gospel of Mark, complete a short-term mission project, or get through a quarter of marriage-enrichment lessons. The groups are minted with a short expiration date stamped on their foreheads, so why become personally invested? Why risk sharing anything deeply personal when the group will disband in a few months?

Of course, asking for a 20-year commitment will elicit a very short list of volunteers. Roy's group—and other groups that last for decades—aren't formed with longevity in mind; it just sort of happens.

But it *does* happen…and if being involved in a long-term small group is such a powerful experience, it's worth considering how your church can encourage more small groups to go the distance—to stay active for more than a year or two.

So how do you do it? How do you design small groups so they have a vibrant, long life? So group members find so much value in their small-group experience that they'll continue meeting year after year?

What's the secret? What does Roy Miller know that you don't know?

THE SECRET OF LONG-LASTING, LIFE-GIVING SMALL GROUPS

Ready?

The fact is there *isn't* a secret…not really.

What held Roy Miller's share group together for decades is pretty much what holds every *other* small group together: a healthy dose of trust, a clear purpose, and a willingness to move toward transparency. And then there are those *additional* ingredients: The group experience has to be relevant and sufficiently beneficial so that it's worth an ongoing investment.

Here's what Roy says about his long-lived share group and why it worked so well.

THEY BEGAN AS FRIENDS

Roy's original group was composed of people who for the most part already knew and liked each other. Most of the faces Roy saw at his first meeting were familiar.

There *are* dangers of launching a small group that includes best buddies—at least, if you want the group to grow. New people can find it tough to penetrate an existing network of friendships. If there's such strong shared history that new people feel out of place, they won't stay long. See page 93 for solutions to this problem.

Still, there's something to be said for starting a small group with people who already know each other. They don't have to make the progression from "stranger" to "acquaintance" to "friend." They can start right at "friend" and move toward "trusted friend." And until group members trust each other, they won't share what's really happening in their lives.

> **WE'RE STILL IN TOUCH WITH PEOPLE WHO MOVED AWAY YEARS AGO. WE SHARED A POWERFUL TIME IN OUR LIVES AND THOSE OF OUR CHILDREN, AND WE'RE ALL GRATEFUL FOR IT.**
> —ROY MILLER

An additional plus to tapping into friendships when launching small groups is that people probably already spend time together. They stand on the same sidelines at their kids' soccer games, get together for coffee, and chat while standing in line at the bank or grocery store.

In some cases, group members might even work together.

"I ended up working with some of my small-group members," says Roy. *That* certainly accelerated relationships!

THEY KEPT IT SIMPLE AND STUCK TO THEIR PURPOSE

At their first monthly meeting, the families in Roy's group gathered in a home. Each family brought a dish to pass, and after everyone had eaten dinner, the kids took off to play together. Adults cleared the tables and sat with cups of coffee, talking.

"We started with an icebreaker question, I think," remembers Roy. "Then we just talked. When something came up that we could pray about, that's what we did." After several hours families gathered up their kids and went home.

The format worked so well the group repeated it at the second meeting. And the third. And, for the most part, at every meeting thereafter.

"We rotated homes, we always had a potluck meal, and the host family facilitated the meeting," says Roy. "It doesn't get much simpler."

Through the years Roy's group seldom used a devotional guide or other study aid. "We weren't primarily a Bible study," says Roy. "We were meeting to live out our lives together, and we didn't need curriculum for that."

If the lack of Bible study frightens you, remember: The members of Roy's group were already Christians. They were active in church. They were regularly hearing what the Bible says; where they wanted and needed help was living their faith.

"Don't get me wrong," Roy is quick to say, "We never let our meetings become just social affairs. We always had at least an hour of sharing and prayer."

Simple is good. Purposeful is even better.

THEY PRAYED TOGETHER—OFTEN

"We called it a share group," remembers Roy. "That pretty much set the expectation that people were encouraged to talk. At first it was mostly women sharing things while we men were quiet, hanging back. It took a few months for the guys to open up."

What prompted the men to join in, says Roy, was seeing God actually answering prayers.

From the very beginning, prayer was a central part of the group's time together. And not the "I'll pray about it when I get home" sort of prayer; when something came up in discussion, it was prayed about on the spot.

"By the time we'd prayed together for six months and seen how God responded, we'd bonded in serious ways," says Roy. "When people have prayed with you and then seen how God answered, that builds relationships."

THEY KEPT IT SMALL

"We started with four or five couples and kept the group about that size through the years," says Roy. When the group grew larger, it was divided into two groups.

The small size made it possible to know not only the couples who attended, but their children and life situations as well.

Through the years, some members of Roy's group moved away. One at a time, several families relocated from Denver to California or elsewhere—and it was always a significant experience for the group.

"We felt it every time someone left," says Miller. "They weren't just people we knew from the neighborhood or from church. They were family."

Before inviting others to join, Roy's group had met for several years. By that time the relationships were cemented and secure, and everyone knew what to expect from meeting to meeting. Inviting other couples to attend meant that the group would divide, but sharing the positive community was worth it to Roy and his friends.

> **MY INVOLVEMENT IN OUR SHARE GROUP HAS BEEN ONE OF THE MOST ENRICHING EXPERIENCES OF MY LIFE. GETTING TOGETHER WITH PEOPLE OVER THE COURSE OF YEARS, HAVING OUR CHILDREN GROW UP TOGETHER, SHARING UPS AND DOWNS—IT'S BEEN SIMPLE, BUT IT'S MET PROFOUND NEEDS.**
> —ROY MILLER

You'll note that Roy's share group was a *couples* group. It was intentionally geared to married couples. Singles weren't invited, though when one couple divorced, the wife remained. "We were a support for her," remembers Roy. "Her husband left, but she needed us. We weren't about to kick out either of them."

Small groups that include dozens of people are unlikely to experience deep community. You simply can't be intimately involved in the lives of that many people at once.

THEY KEPT IT SAFE

Roy's group was able to be honest and transparent in part because what was shared in the group *remained* in the group. That was an expectation expressed early and often.

Did an assurance that it was safe to share prompt open discussion?

No, but that sort of assurance seldom does.

"After we'd met for a few months and personal things weren't repeated outside the group, that's when we began to share intimately," says Roy.

In other words, it takes time and testing. Another benefit of a long-term share group is that community comes only after everyone decides it's possible.

THEY INCLUDED THE ENTIRE FAMILY

If you're going to live out life together, it's natural to include the whole family. If small-group members don't know one another's children, they're disconnected from a large part of their lives.

"Our children actually grew up together," says Roy. "One couple with grown children became surrogate grandparents. They'd sometimes keep kids for the weekend so a couple could get away together."

The bonds that formed between children in the group became as strong as those forged by the parents. "My son and the son of another couple are still best friends," says Roy, "and they're grown men now."

In what became a tradition, the couples in Roy's group set aside Memorial Day weekend for a group vacation. Between five and 10 families rented cabins at a lake, and the entire herd spent the weekend together. "We'd cook out and eat together in the evening, and we had a great time sharing and playing together. On Sunday we'd all pile in cars and go to a local church as a group."

After a few couples moved to California, several Memorial Day weekends became road trips. "We all flew out from Denver to visit our expatriate members," remembers Roy with a chuckle.

THEY SERVED EACH OTHER IN PRACTICAL WAYS

Some of the best moments of living life together happened not at the monthly meetings, but as group members helped each other with projects.

Painting a house. Putting in a garden. Hauling rock for landscaping. Anytime a group member could use a hand became an excuse for serving each other and sharing.

Roy remembers a time his family moved from one house in Denver to another. "The share group showed up with pickup trucks, and we spent the day loading and unloading them. One woman brought a huge pot of chili that kept us fed all day long as we worked together."

Perhaps it's obvious, but what causes a group to thrive for decades is pretty much what causes a group to last for any length of time: a shared purpose, transparency, and relevance. What's different about long-lived groups is that they normally include settled people who aren't relocating. And the groups are designed to remove obstacles to longevity.

STEPS

If you want the small groups in your church to stay together longer, here are some practical steps to take:

IDENTIFY THE LONG-LASTING SMALL GROUPS THAT ALREADY EXIST

Start your search with senior citizen Sunday school classes. In some churches they're remarkably stable, and their relationships extend outside the classroom. Talk with class members. What insights do they have about creating community? Why are they close? You're likely to find they have shared history, they rely on each other for practical things, and they feel free to talk about current life issues. Their relationships are relevant and vital.

FOCUS ON SHARING LIFE, NOT LESSONS

> **When word got out that we were forming life groups that would give people the chance to talk about real-world stuff, I was mobbed. People are hungry for relationships.**
> —Greg Sanders

"In our church we have lots of groups based around activities and very few based around life together," says Greg Sanders, a Colorado associate pastor and worship leader. "I don't need another activity. I need life."

So Greg put out the word that anyone interested in a small group that leaned more toward experiencing life together and away from a quarterly Bible study should meet for a potluck on a Friday night.

Enough people showed up at the first meeting to launch two groups.

Greg is deliberate in his "no lesson books" approach to his group. "We need to talk and pray together," he says. "I don't want to sound snobbish, but the last thing I want is to be all churchy in our small group. I want to know what's happening in lives. I want to be close enough to people that they know me and can hold me accountable for things in my life and marriage."

ENCOURAGE MEMBERSHIP, BUT PROVIDE AN EXIT RAMP

As people cycle into a group, build in opt-out moments.

Some group members have no idea what it means to share their lives, to speak honestly to each other, to be accountable. And when they make that discovery, some of them want out.

Rather than putting people in a position in which they feel compelled to make excuses, clearly mark the exit ramps. Moving out of the country is certainly one, but there are others.

"We don't want small groups to be a burden," Greg says. "But they shouldn't be something you can just walk away from, either. It's important to know that someone's not running away."

Roy thinks it's important to give new people time to see if it the small group is what they truly want.

"Whenever someone new joined our group, we met together for a month and then talked about whether the group was meeting everyone's needs," he says. "By then everyone—including the couple deciding whether to join—knew if the group was a fit."

HELP NEW PEOPLE FIND A HOME

To help new people make connections within an existing group that's been together for years, do the following:

- Clarify expectations about confidentiality. Maybe the need for confidentiality is understood by veteran group members, but the new people need to know that their vulnerability is as valued as that of veterans.
- Stick with your regular format. During times new people are considering making a commitment to the group, do what you normally do. New members need to see what kind of life group they're joining. What's safe to discuss? What's unsafe?
- Tell your faith stories. It may be ground that's been covered among the veterans, but even they will be encouraged to hear again what God's done in the lives of others.

FINAL THOUGHTS ABOUT...HOW THE CHURCH CAN HELP

The forces that shorten small-group life are alive and well. Group members move away. People change churches. A shift in church focus might urge church members to meet in groups designed to support outreach or missions or parenting or marriage. Groups disband when a quarter's curriculum is completed.

To survive for years, what groups most need from the church is for the church to pray for them but to otherwise simply leave them alone. To honor their desire to live honestly and with integrity in full view of others. To do peer ministry that can only be done by trusted friends. To be there for each other in times of trouble and moments of joy.

To be the church.

"A FRIEND IS SOMEONE WHO UNDERSTANDS YOUR PAST, BELIEVES IN YOUR FUTURE, AND ACCEPTS YOU TODAY JUST THE WAY YOU ARE. A FRIEND IS SOMEONE WITH WHOM YOU DARE TO BE YOURSELF."
—C. RAYMOND BERAN

BUILD COMMUNITY THROUGH MEMBERSHIP RETREATS

This church has found a way to increase membership and nurture community at the same time.

☑ DEEPENS MEMBERS' COMMITMENT TO CHRIST AND THE CHURCH'S MISSION

☑ CREATES LONG-LASTING CONNECTIONS AMONG NEW MEMBERS

☑ COMMUNICATES THE VISION OF THE CHURCH

☑ WORKS FOR CHURCHES OF ANY SIZE

A COUNTERCULTURAL APPROACH

In a culture that demonstrates growing resistance to the gospel message and commitment to the church, Chapel Hill Presbyterian Church in Gig Harbor, Washington, is challenging these trends with counterintuitive methods that are transforming lives. Chapel Hill requires prospective members to attend a weekend retreat called "Welcome to the Family," in which the claims of Christ are explored, the mission of the church is explained, and prospective members who haven't accepted Christ are invited to do so. In the process, a special kind of community forms, stemming from shared involvement in an intense experience and a common commitment to life-changing goals.

In the late 1980s, Senior Pastor Mark Toone began serving this congregation, which at that time numbered 185. The church taught a standard membership class over a five-week period, but the class did little more than disseminate information. It didn't allow attendees to process any of what they'd heard, and it did nothing to foster community among them. Most of them forgot the information as soon as the class ended.

In 1987, Mark began experimenting with an alternative membership class. He wanted to provide an experience that would be meaningful on several levels. First, he hoped to convey the church's love for its people. Second, he was determined to communicate the gospel message in clear and definite terms. Third, he wanted participants to gain a deeper understanding of Chapel Hill's vision and the church's expectations of its members. Finally, he hoped that these elements would work together to deepen new members' commitment to Christ, to the church, and to one another. Over time, Welcome to the Family has come to achieve all of these goals.

WHY MEMBERSHIP?

The church's mission statement reads, "The mission of Chapel Hill is to present everyone mature in Christ." Mark Toone has concluded, "If we are going to accomplish this mission, one of the keys is membership."

Why? According to Executive Pastor Stuart Bond, "Members are more committed; members volunteer more; members give more." They share the church's desire to influence others through the love of Christ.

While many churches are backing off on a call to church membership, Chapel Hill has chosen to emphasize its importance. Stuart admits, "I know a call to membership is countercultural, but we *pound* it."

The church's leaders express great confidence in this emphasis. They promote membership as a central part of their worship services. In fact, on the Sunday following each membership retreat, the attendees of the retreats, along with all the other church members, are asked to stand and recite their membership commitments during the worship services. This leaves the nonmembers—about one-fifth of the congregation—seated and watching. The leadership team recognizes that this might make nonmembers feel uncomfortable. Stuart is unapologetic, saying, "They will either remain uncomfortable, or they will join the church."

Because the church doesn't want its people to sit on the sidelines, receiving ministry without ministering to others, it's not backing off its emphasis on membership.

MARK'S ALLERGY

Another reason Mark moved away from the didactic membership-class model was his recognition that some members of the church didn't really know what it meant to be a Christian. He realized that too many people had said that they knew Jesus and had become members when in reality they had never given their lives to Christ. Mark states, "I am allergic to this."

As a result, a primary component of Welcome to the Family is a gospel presentation. There is nothing unique about it; church leaders use the four spiritual laws. What is special is that they *do* it. They begin by demonstrating that church membership is founded upon Christ and a personal relationship with him.

At every retreat, five or six of the 30 or so people in attendance give their lives to Christ for the first time. In fact, Mark has seen elders from other churches pray to receive Christ in this setting. At one membership retreat, a retired Presbyterian minister realized that he had spent his entire career preaching something that he had never personally embraced. He accepted Christ for the first time.

However, the decision to follow Christ is not forced upon prospective members. They aren't asked to walk down an aisle or raise their hands. Instead, most people who pray to receive Christ at this time do so in small-group settings or in private conversations with other individuals.

THE IMPORTANCE OF SMALL GROUPS

The leadership of Chapel Hill understands that if people don't have a chance to process what they hear, they won't retain it. And if they aren't encouraged to apply the truths they've heard to their own situations, their lives will remain unchanged. As you can see from the "Five Gs" below and on the next page, the church asks prospective members to investigate profound commitments—commitments that, if embraced, will change their lives forever.

It is not enough to explain the church's vision; prospective members must have a chance to grapple with every aspect of it. That is why, during the retreat, people are placed in small groups, in which they are encouraged to process what they're learning. At the Sunday service following each retreat, new members are asked to recite their membership commitments aloud. Without adequate processing, promises to support the vision would be empty indeed. For all of these reasons, the membership retreats rely heavily on a small-group format. And vital to the success of any small group is a good facilitator.

The Five Gs

Chapel Hill Presbyterian Church's membership retreats are organized around the "Five Gs" of the church's vision: glorify, gather, grapple, give, and go.

- **GLORIFY—A call from self to God**
A daily encounter with an awesome God
Commitment: "I promise to love God with all my heart."
Romans 12:1

- **GATHER—A call from isolation to community**
An invitation into intimate Christian community
Commitment: "I promise to worship at Chapel Hill regularly and to share my life with others in this church family."
Hebrews 10:24

- **GRAPPLE—A call from denial to honesty**
A biblical, honest, and hope-filled engagement with the issues of life
Commitment: "I promise to wrestle with life's challenges while holding on to Jesus."
Colossians 1:29; 2 Thessalonians 2:15-17; 2 Timothy 2:14-26

(Continued on following page.)

(Continued from previous page.)

• GIVE—A call from hoarding to trusting

A joyful dedication of selves and resources to the cause of the kingdom

Commitment: *"I promise to be obedient to God's claim on my money and my talents for his work at Chapel Hill."*

Matthew 10:8b

• GO—A call from here to there

A resolve to break out of comfort zones into the world with the love of Christ

Commitment: *"I promise to stretch myself to reach others with God's love and truth."*

Matthew 28:18-20

FACILITATORS

Stuart admits that finding good facilitators has been a matter of trial and error. Some people have a propensity for asking stimulating questions and engaging people in dialogue; many others don't. Facilitators must possess these qualities as well as good listening skills and the ability to connect quickly with a group of people, as there is little time to waste during a short retreat. (Welcome to the Family begins on Friday evening and lasts all day Saturday.)

John Hanson is the volunteer who coordinates Welcome to the Family. Before he assumed this role, the pastors were continually scrambling to find facilitators. John not only has a passion for this ministry, he also has a special eye for finding good facilitators.

A Good Small-Group Facilitator Is...

- *committed to God*
- *enthusiastically supportive of the vision of the church*
- *passionate about connecting people*
- *genuinely interested in people's stories*
- *able to ask questions that invite conversation*
- *quick to smile and laugh*
- *able to get people to open up*
- *available on weekends and willing to attend retreats regularly*

A GLIMPSE INTO THE WEEKEND

One of the strengths of the retreat is the consistent demonstration that the church genuinely cares about the people in attendance. Participants are treated to meals, and competent child care is provided throughout the retreat. All of the church's pastors participate in the retreat at some point. These gestures demonstrate that the church sincerely values its new members.

The retreat begins on Friday evening. From 7:00 to 8:30 p.m., Mark Toone explores the first G of the church's mission: to glorify God. He asks, "Who is Jesus?" Common misconceptions about Jesus and Christianity are explored. Finally, he invites prospective members who haven't made faith commitments to consider doing so.

Saturday begins at 8:30 with a continental breakfast, followed by a devotion given by Stuart. Then participants begin to get acquainted through an interactive icebreaker. From 10:00 until 11:45, another pastor explores the second G in the church's mission: to gather with other Christians. In this context, the pastor discusses the church's views on baptism and the Lord's Supper, and other staff members describe some of the ways new members might consider becoming involved in the life of the church.

Lunch is served from 11:45 to 12:30 and is followed by a discussion of the third G of the church's mission: to grapple with life's challenges while relying on Jesus. The pastor explores the idea of spiritual maturity and steps Christians can take toward it.

After an afternoon break and class photo, another pastor explores the fourth G: what it means to give one's time, talent, and resources to the cause of Christ. Then the church's director of missions and emerging ministries discusses the fifth G of the church's mission: to go into the world, to stretch in order to reach others.

From 3:00 to 4:00, participants are encouraged to share their personal faith journeys in small groups. After people have connected around the content of the retreat, enough trust has usually been established to allow them to talk about their spiritual journeys. Concluding the retreat with this kind of intimate sharing communicates that living in community is central to the vision and mission of the church. Talking about the importance of authentic relationships in the church is of limited value—usually of no value—if people don't actually experience them there.

The final step in the process occurs on Sunday, when new members stand during the church's worship services and, joined by all of the other members, recite the commitments they have made as members of Chapel Hill Presbyterian Church. It's a powerful moment, and it's repeated five times each year. It goes a long way toward deepening and solidifying this church's sense of community and commitment to the body of Christ.

Frequency

> *Chapel Hill holds membership retreats five times each year. In one of them, the church includes youth who are about to be confirmed.*

AFTER THE RETREAT

To help participants in the retreats live out their membership commitments, a deacon visits each new member one month after Welcome to the Family. This is one way the church cares for its members and one of its first steps in discipleship.

Because Chapel Hill values community life, the church also encourages the small groups that were formed at the retreat to accept a "Four-Week Challenge." The groups are invited to meet for four weeks to explore material provided by the church. By doing this, the church hopes the groups will deepen their connections and continue to meet after the four weeks are over.

The Four-Week Challenge has met with varying levels of success. It has worked well with some groups. For others, the connections have seemed forced, especially among those who had attended the retreat after years of involvement in the church. They were already connected, and the small group wasn't a natural way to advance their community life within the church.

As a result, the pastors are experimenting with other ways of getting people connected. They are emphasizing a more personal and organic approach, helping new people plug into existing groups or continue to attend small groups to which they had previously belonged. After leading more than 2,000 people through Welcome to the Family over nearly 20 years, Chapel Hill continues to experiment with ways to connect people within the church.

EXPERIMENTING WITH AN ALTERNATIVE TO THE RETREAT

One key ingredient to the success of Welcome to the Family is the retreat format. It is intense and concentrated. It promotes a progression of transparency and spiritual momentum. At the same time, the church's leaders have received feedback that the retreat format hinders many committed individuals from becoming members because their schedules prevent them from attending a weekend event.

The church is therefore experimenting with an alternative that would allow participants to meet one evening a week for five weeks. Mark is quick to emphasize that this alternative will continue to stress small-group interaction and in-depth exploration of the tenets of Christianity. And he hopes that over the course of the five weeks, participants will experience the progressive transparency and spiritual momentum that have characterized the retreat format.

CHAPTER NINE
IMPLEMENTATION

GUIDELINES

If you find yourself thinking that this pattern might work in your church, Stuart admits that this approach is neither novel nor difficult. But if you follow certain guidelines, your chances of success will be much greater.

1. **Secure the endorsement of the church's key leaders.** They must place a high value on membership. Stuart advises that you begin with your primary lay leadership body. If you don't secure this group's commitment, the process will never work.

2. **Assure consistent involvement by pastoral staff members.** Their active involvement in every retreat will go a long way toward demonstrating the church's commitment to the principle of membership as well as to its members.

3. **Identify, recruit, and train good facilitators.** During your first retreat, the members of lay leadership might serve in this capacity, but don't expect all of them to be good facilitators. Select those with a gift for facilitating, and continue to recruit for the next retreat. Refine this process as you go. Making it a priority will help ensure its success.

4. **Promote the new process of membership to the church body.** After explaining the new approach to the church, expect lots of questions and perhaps some resistance. Don't argue too much for the validity of the new format; rather, let the results speak for themselves. The best form of promotion will be the personal testimonies of the new members. After a few retreats, use their experiences to promote the idea to others.

5. **Require prospective members to attend the entire retreat.** If your goals for the retreat are to deepen participants' understanding of the claims of Christ, to secure their commitment to the goals of the church, and to help them form bonds of friendship, their involvement in every step is crucial. Make it clear that membership depends upon attending all of the sessions.

6. **Make sure the topics are relevant and are taught in fresh, engaging ways.** Nothing will doom a membership retreat faster than boring content. The claims of Christ are revolutionary, unique, and countercultural. Present them in such a way that prospective members realize all over again how truly awesome our God is. Use teaching methods that are relational, experiential, applicable, and learner-based. Find ways to make the content unforgettable!

7. **Ask for honest feedback, and learn from your mistakes.** Your church will improve with each retreat, but only if it seeks and listens to feedback.

FINAL THOUGHTS ABOUT...SWIMMING AGAINST THE TIDE

All churches—regardless of their size and traditions—can make church membership a priority. While this notion does challenge the assumptions of our culture, it might be just the kind of challenge the culture needs. Mark says, "We can attribute our numerical growth to the fact that we have chosen to focus on membership."

> "YOU ARE NO LONGER FOREIGNERS AND ALIENS, BUT FELLOW CITIZENS WITH GOD'S PEOPLE AND MEMBERS OF GOD'S HOUSEHOLD, BUILT ON THE FOUNDATION OF THE APOSTLES AND PROPHETS, WITH CHRIST JESUS HIMSELF AS THE CHIEF CORNERSTONE."
> —EPHESIANS 2:19-20

BUILD COMMUNITY WITH COLLEGE STUDENTS

This church reaches out to college students on Valentine's Day with care packages that remind students they're loved.

☑ EASY TO IMPLEMENT

☑ WORKS FOR CHURCHES OF ANY SIZE

☑ BUILDS INTERGENERATIONAL COMMUNITY

☑ SEASONAL

BEING REMEMBERED

It was a cold February day several years ago when Casey Keepers checked her mailbox after class at Nyack College.

Tucked in with the stack of credit card offers and school notices was something Casey didn't expect: a slip of paper. A slip of pink paper. A pink slip of paper that meant—somewhere behind the counter at the college post office—a package was waiting with her name on it.

"I stood in line wondering who could possibly be sending me something," Casey says. "Then the whole time I was walking back to my dorm room, I kept trying to pry the box open with my keys."

Casey still remembers what came tumbling out of the box. "There were all sorts of school supplies—markers, highlighters, pencils—all the stuff I'd been running out of. There were some homemade cookies, too.

"And best of all—a Valentine and letter from my youth group back home."

As much as Casey appreciated the supplies and food, it was the letter she remembers. "It felt nice because while I was away at school, I was missing out on lots of stuff I used to do with our group. The letter was a reminder that I was missed. They remembered me."

As surprised as Casey was to discover a box waiting for her at the post office that Valentine's Day, here's something she'd have found even more amazing: Casey wasn't alone.

That same day, 25 *other* college students opened similar Valentine's Day care boxes, on a dozen different college campuses.

Surprise: Preakness Baptist Church had struck again.

VALENTINE'S DAY CARE BOXES

Each winter, folks at Preakness Baptist Church in Wayne, New Jersey, collect goodies and ship them to college students—and not just college students who happen to be church members. Boxes *also* arrive on the doorsteps of students who have visited the church a time or two. Students who've attended a retreat or class sponsored by the church. Students who've been recommended to the church because they have no family nearby and could use some encouragement.

What motivates the effort isn't a desire to feed hungry students, though that certainly happens. The church's intent is to build community—and it works.

"The first place we build community is in our own congregation," says Jane Harlan, Preakness' youth pastor. "It's a team effort, and that draws together our people in creating the boxes.

"This is also a reminder to our people that we're part of a larger community. The church of Jesus Christ is bigger than our own four walls and includes people who aren't our church members."

The boxes prompt community on the receiving end, too. The care boxes create *instant* community when they're opened and the smell of homemade cookies wafts through the dorm. The scent of chocolate chip cookies draws students faster than free concert tickets.

Valentine boxes arrive packed to the brim—the better to encourage recipients to share their goodies with roommates and dorm neighbors. A box of doughnuts and bag of chips are built-in excuses for connecting with fellow students. Few things build relationships—and community—as quickly as sharing.

Preakness Baptist Church isn't a large church; about 130 people come on any given Sunday morning. That means collecting enough stuff to fill 25 or 30 boxes each February is a daunting task. At least, you might think so.

But you'd be wrong.

TEN YEARS AND COUNTING

"We started sending Valentine boxes to college students 10 years ago—the year we had 20 kids in our youth group leave for college," Jane remembers. "When 20 kids disappear from a group of 75, you feel it. We wanted kids who left to know we still loved and cared for them."

And, she thought, how better to say it than with snacks and a Valentine's Day card?

The first year Jane pulled together the program, it took a bit of explaining. "Our congregation is very giving," says Jane. "We have lots of opportunities to give throughout the year. But sending snacks to college students? There was enthusiasm for the project, but I had to connect this project with the larger values of caring and sharing God's love."

Now the program has become part of Preakness' DNA. "Everyone gets involved," says Jane. "Especially the senior citizens."

THE SENIOR-SENIOR CONNECTION

It's no accident that senior citizens support students at Preakness. Jane has been intentional about connecting junior and high school students with older members of the congregation—especially those who are 60 and older.

"Every year we have a retreat for our junior highers," says Jane. "We always bring four or five widows from our congregation with us on the retreat. They're lonely, and they have so much to offer our young people. Participating in a retreat cements the relationships between the kids and senior adults.

> **THIS PROGRAM IS MEANINGFUL TO OUR OLDER ADULTS. WHEN JANUARY ROLLS AROUND, THEY ASK ME WHEN I'M GOING TO GET GOING ON THE PROJECT.**
> —JANE HARLAN

"During the course of the year, our young people send notes and birthday cards to the older members of our congregation. That builds relationships and respect in both directions, and one place you see how powerfully the young and old have bonded is when it's time to create Valentine boxes.

"One lady baked hundreds of little muffins last year—it was remarkable."

Jane begins collecting items right after New Year's Day, asking the congregation for items college students will appreciate. "The donations range from homemade cookies and other packaged snacks to quarters for dorm washing machines. We get office supplies, too—pencils, paper—and anything else a student might need."

Collections continue throughout January. Then, the week before Valentine's Day, junior and senior high youth groups put the items in boxes. "We send boxes everywhere—all over the country," Jane says. "We drop a note in each box, seal it up with tape, and ship it off."

Well…*some* boxes get shipped.

Others go on a road trip.

ROAD TRIP

Whenever possible, Jane prefers the personal touch of delivering the boxes in person. It's not unusual for Jane and one or two of her team to drive several hours to place a box in the hands of a college student. Still, they've had to draw the line.

"A few years ago a student was in England during spring semester," Jane remembers. "*That* was a bit far to travel in person.

"It cost $30 to ship the box, but the student was so touched. He was away from home and lonely, and for that box to show up—to communicate that we hadn't forgotten him and we were thinking of him—was great. We got a beautiful note from him.

"He said, 'I shared my box with so many people—and they could hardly believe my church would spend so much money sending me treats. I knew that I was loved.' "

SEEING THE IMPACT

Many college students return for Preakness' annual all-youth retreat. That's one time Jane sees the impact of the Valentine boxes.

"We've had kids bring friends with them," says Jane. "The friends saw how our church loved their roommates or friends, and that draws them. Each year three or four college kids come whom we've never met—but they met our cookies and our people."

CARE BOXES: NOT *JUST* FOR COLLEGE STUDENTS ANYMORE

Jane has adapted this program and has sent care packages to church members who are serving in the armed forces.

"One of our members was serving in Iraq. I wrote up a list of things he'd like to receive and let the congregation know. They supplied every item on the list. I also asked for letters. He must have received at least 50 of them. He later told me that he just sat there, in Iraq, reading all the letters one by one."

Jane's church also sends kids and adult volunteers to a Group Workcamp—a weeklong service project in the summer. Early on, each participant makes a list of the snacks he or she enjoys, with the caveat that nothing on the list can be perishable.

> **"I DON'T HAVE TO BRING ANY SNACKS TO WORK-CAMP. WE END UP WITH SO MANY SNACKS THAT OUR KIDS CAN HELP CREATE COMMUNITY BY SHARING WHAT THEY HAVE WITH OTHERS."**
> **—JANE HARLAN**

Then, on Memorial Day weekend, each Workcamp volunteer is "adopted" by someone in the church. The adopter might be a friend or a friend of the family, or there may be no direct connection at all—yet.

The day before the youth group leaves for Workcamp, a bag appears for each camper. Tucked inside are that camper's favorite snacks and drinks, plus all the sundries teenagers are notorious for forgetting: suntan lotion, disposable cameras, toothbrushes, and tubes of toothpaste. Plus, each camper sets out for camp with an encouraging note.

IMPLEMENTATION

GETTING STARTED

Here's how Jane pulls together the Valentine's College Care Package program each year. Consider this a template if you'd like to start a similar program in your church.

IT'S ALL ABOUT RELATIONSHIPS

Establish relationships between the youth and adults in your church *before* asking adults to chip in to create college-bound care packages. "On Valentine's Day our youth sponsor a dinner after church for senior citizens," says Jane.

While her motivation isn't to soften up seniors for donations, the following year their willingness to jump in and participate is a happy consequence.

ADVERTISE

Jane drops an announcement in the bulletin to get the ball rolling.

"I make an announcement the week after New Year's Day," says Jane. "I say it's time to start thinking about our College Care packages, time to send our love to all our youth who are away at college."

That's all the nudge it takes to get the program underway, though Jane keeps people posted by dropping an update in the bulletin each week during January.

"I may say, 'Reminder: College kids love Doritos.'"

MAKE A LIST...AND CHECK IT TWICE

"I track the kids," says Jane. "I have all their e-mail addresses, and I keep posted on who's in school and who's graduated."

This takes less effort than you might expect. Jane's an avid e-mailer, so staying connected is something she enjoys, and there's not a college student alive who's not connected electronically.

Jane keeps tabs on who's in school for another reason. "We keep a roster in our church directory," she says. "Our church members know every college student who's away."

And to be included on the directory's college page, a student doesn't have to be a church member. Jane lists every student who's been involved with the church during the past four years. They may have come to a retreat or attended a class or simply visited.

"We want to pray for college students because it's a challenging time in their lives. Keeping their names in front of our people is one way to encourage that prayer."

BE GENEROUS WITH WHOM YOU INCLUDE

It's a given: When students graduate from high school and head off to college, they often stop going to church. That's true even if they live in Mom's basement and attend the local junior college.

They still get a basket.

"We never make church attendance a prerequisite for receiving a box," says Jane. "We encourage students to connect with churches and programs where they're studying. We love seeing students when they're back in town visiting, but they need to be active while they're away, too."

But whether a student is attending church weekly while at school or is sleeping through Sundays, that student receives a care box.

Jane says, "I've never taken a student off the list—never.

"Sometimes college kids take their own road for a few years. We continue to pray for them, and we stay in touch. We let them know we're thinking about them and ask that they let us know if they need something. Sometimes I'll get a note letting me know that they've come back to church—though not necessarily ours—and that they appreciate that we never stopped caring."

It's important to note that students don't actually have to be *away* at school to receive a box. Students who happen to be living at home and attending college still get a package...as do adults who are enrolled in college.

"If you're 40 and you've gone back for your masters—you'll get a package," says Jane, who laughs as she points out *she's* going back to college next year—and she's expecting a package, too.

RECRUIT HELP WITH SHIPPING

At Preakness, the junior and senior high Sunday school classes assemble the boxes. It just makes sense; they're personally invested in keeping the program running.

"They know *they're* going to get boxes eventually," says Jane. "Seniors say, 'I can't wait to go away next year so I can get a box.'"

STANDARDIZE THE BOXES

Jane doesn't cut corners on boxes. She buys new cardboard boxes at an office supply store for about a dollar per box. It's worth the expense.

"One year we used shoeboxes—we don't do that anymore. Even though we wrapped them carefully, they're not as sturdy."

The boxes Jane buys are slightly larger than a shoebox. "You could fit a pair of boots in them," she says. The actual size of the box isn't as important as the fact that the boxes are identical.

"When you have five kids in the same college getting a box, those boxes had better be the same size," Jane says.

Shipping costs are about $5.50 per box—though shipping to England or another distant location will certainly raise the price considerably. Jane sends the boxes through the regular postal service, and they've always arrived in good shape.

INCLUDE A VALENTINE NOTE

The senior and junior highers write a note to include in each box. Notes are straightforward and affirming. "Usually students write something like, 'Here's your Valentine. We hope you know we care about you,' " says Jane.

While she's never quite certain what a student will write, the fact that the note is personalized makes the risk worthwhile. Besides, Jane makes sure teenagers penning the notes understand their cards *will* be read and should be encouraging.

DON'T WAIT BY THE MAILBOX

"I don't expect a response," Jane says, "but I often hear something back by e-mail. I'll get notes telling me that the boxes were really great or that someone's roommates loved the box."

Sometimes Jane hears from college students who have drifted away from the church and who weren't expecting a Valentine box. "There was one girl who'd stepped away from our church, and when she got the box it touched her," says Jane. "I got a card from her saying, 'You have no idea what that did for me.' "

Jane posts thank-you e-mail responses on the church bulletin board so everyone can read them. "People want to know they're having an impact," she says.

CHOOSE ITEMS CAREFULLY

Some items travel better than others. Some snacks are more universally loved than others. Stick with snacks that don't leak, crush, or curdle quickly. And be certain that individual treats are wrapped tightly.

Remember that a prepaid phone card or extra stack of coins for the Laundromat are always appreciated, too. Treats don't have to be edible...but munchies are often the most welcome.

And if you do send edible goodies, choose those that will be as edible at the end of the journey as they were at the beginning.

"On the practical side, you've got to be careful with chips and chocolate," Jane warns. "We sent a big box of chocolate candy bars to a serviceman in Iraq, and that was a mistake."

Somewhere between New Jersey and Iraq the bunch of individual chocolate bars morphed into one large chocolate puddle...which was still appreciated.

"He said the guys ate them all," Jane laughs.

FIVE EASY WAYS TO ADAPT THIS IDEA

Care packages are welcomed by people who might be wondering if they're truly remembered now that they're no longer attending church every week. Consider adapting this idea by sending packages to the following people in the same situation:

- **Missionaries**—One church in Ohio sends Fourth of July celebration items (red, white, and blue plastic tablecloths and paper plates; banners; and other decorations) to American missionaries serving overseas. Thanksgiving items are equally appreciated. Plan ahead, though—packages can take up to a month to reach distant locations

- **Retirees**—They've moved to Florida, but that doesn't mean they'll quickly make friends or connect with a local congregation. Remind them that their faithful involvement in your congregation is honored and remembered—and that God has a place for them in another local church where they've moved.

- **The homebound**—Whether they've suffered a broken leg or recently welcomed triplets, people who are home for an extended period of time need to be reminded that they're not forgotten.

- **Those in retirement homes**—Personal care items and small gifts that will easily fit in a one-room apartment are reminders of home to those who have entered this stage of their lives.

- **Military personnel**—Men and women from your congregation serving in the military face danger every day, and they especially appreciate reminders that their church families are supporting them in prayer.

"WITHOUT A SENSE OF CARING,
THERE CAN BE NO SENSE OF COMMUNITY."
—ANTHONY D'ANGELO

CHAPTER ELEVEN
BUILD COMMUNITY THROUGH DATE NIGHTS

By providing child care and other practical help,
this church helps married couples enrich their marriages.

- ☑ MODERATELY EASY TO IMPLEMENT
- ☑ WORKS FOR CHURCHES OF ANY SIZE
- ☑ FOSTERS INTERGENERATIONAL COMMUNITY
- ☑ REQUIRES CHILD CARE PROVIDERS

THE END OF DATING

When Peter and Anissa Lay began dating, it seemed there were endless opportunities to spend time together.

Like many couples, nearly *anything* became a date: catching a movie, doing laundry, running errands, fixing a meal—as long as they were together and had the chance to talk, their time together counted as a date.

And it was fairly easy to find time to talk after they were married, too. The months and years drifted along with no shortage of dates—as long as they defined *date* broadly.

Then Brennen arrived—a 6-pound, 2-ounce date-dasher.

"We'd moved to Missouri," explains Anissa, "and we didn't have family nearby to help out. Since we're particular about who watches Brennen, we didn't go on dates nearly as often."

Early on, Peter and Anissa had set a goal of having a date night twice each month. But after Brennen showed up, what had seemed easily doable suddenly became very complicated.

Dates were no longer spontaneous, grab-your-coat-and-let's-go affairs. They turned into events that required the precise planning of a military campaign: There were baby-sitting troops to line up, supply lines to establish, and—of course—a price tag to consider. Reliable baby-sitting doesn't come cheap. "Several times we skipped dates simply because of the expense," says Anissa.

Squeezed by the baby-sitting expenses and frustrated by the challenge of finding baby sitters they trusted, Peter and Anissa were pretty much left with renting videos, popping up some corn, and watching movies after Brennen was down for the night.

Some date nights.

SECOND BAPTIST TO THE RESCUE

Daryl Eldridge, pastor of Second Baptist Church in Springfield, Missouri, could see what was happening to young couples like the Lays.

Forced to juggle their commitments to marriage, church, careers, and children, couples were scrambling to keep all the plates spinning. And as they juggled priorities, it seemed the plate dropped most often was their investing time in each other.

"We saw that couples needed to spend time together," Daryl says, "and part of why they weren't doing so was a lack of dependable, affordable child care."

Daryl knew where excellent child care was available: their church. A volunteer staff provided top-notch child care week after week. Church families trusted the church's nursery and child care staff, and children were accustomed to being in the rooms on Sunday. So why not open up the child care facilities on selected evenings so couples could drop off kids and then leave to go out to dinner, run errands, or catch an early movie?

SUCCESS...SORT OF

The church scheduled five Friday nights per year to open up the nursery and classrooms for children from birth through sixth grade. Parents were expected to drop off children at 6:00 p.m. and pick them up by 9:00 p.m.

The program was a hit: Nearly 150 children were handed over for the three hours, and the church's child care workers provided a program for them. It was a great opportunity for parents to spend some time together and for the church to provide an additional three hours of Christian education to children.

Perfect, right? In terms of participation, yes. In terms of budget, no.

"At first we asked parents to pay $5 per child for the service," says Linda Mohrman, who serves as a church nursery coordinator. "There was a cap of $10 per family, so a family with three children could get three hours of child care for just $10."

Even better, if parents signed up in advance but didn't show up, their payment was rolled over to the next date night. If the parents showed up for all five date nights (one each in October, November, January, February, and April), the money was refunded—the five nights of child care were free.

According to Linda, "The church went way in the hole financially because we were paying the child care workers."

The second year the church hosted date nights, the number of children was capped at 100, and the church kept the money paid by parents. Those funds helped defray the cost of hiring child care workers.

The third year, the program was modified again: The financial arrangements were the same, but the church hosted just three date nights per year.

"We found that was what we could reasonably do," Linda says.

After some personnel changes at Second Baptist, the date night program was set aside, but popular demand brought it back. At this writing, the program has been up and running again for two years—and it's going strong.

SUCCESS...DEFINITELY

Giving parents a few hours to focus on each other wasn't the only motivation for hosting date night child care, reports Daryl, who has since left the church and now serves as president of Rockbridge Seminary.

"We also used the date night as an educational opportunity for couples," he says. "Because parents had to drop off their children at the same time, we had all the parents together at one time. We asked them to stay for 10 minutes, and we did a quick marriage-enrichment session together."

Daryl pulled out his best tips for couples who wanted to grow in their marriages. He talked for a few minutes and then gave couples something to do on their date. "Sometimes it was a conversational tool, such as a question to discuss," says Daryl. "Sometimes it was an activity to complete."

Here are some of the topics he covered:
• how to handle vacations
• dealing with in-laws
• how to fight fair
• date ideas that are feasible during the week
• renewing romance
• finances

Daryl didn't assume that his quick sessions alone would wow the crowd. "We also raffled off door prizes at the time couples were supposed to be there," he says. Prizes included everything from gift certificates for meals to gift certificates for hotel rooms; the prizes were a great incentive to be prompt.

FOUNDATIONAL COMMUNITY BUILDING

Churches that provide date night options for couples are building community at a foundational level by supporting marriages during what is often a stressful time: the years when young children are in the house.

"Going on a date once every few months isn't the solution to rising divorce rates or family instability," says Daryl. "But it helps."

Second Baptist recommends that couples using their child care service build community another way, too: to get together with another couple for double dates.

> **ONCE CHILDREN COME, PARENTS TEND TO INVEST THEIR ENERGY IN THE CHILDREN. THEY SOMETIMES NO LONGER INVEST ENERGY IN EACH OTHER.**
> —DARYL ELDRIDGE

"We encourage couples who are church members to get together with non-Christian neighbors," Linda says. "It isn't a requirement, but it's a chance to do outreach and to be together at the same time."

Some outreach happens simply because inexpensive child care on a Friday night tends to draw attention. Couples from within the church told their neighbors, and soon Second Baptist discovered unchurched families knocking on the church door.

"When you do a program like this, you begin by ministering to couples in your church, but it quickly spreads to the community," Linda says. "People hear about it and want to participate."

Second Baptist encourages the program to grow beyond serving just church members. "It gets parents through the doors," Linda says. Volunteers are certain that the church delivers excellent child care—rooms are clean, the volunteers are ready to receive children, and the ratios of children to volunteers are right on the money. "Parents are trusting us with their children," Linda says, noting that how well the church honors that trust makes a huge impression. It can determine if a family returns on Sunday.

So date nights can build community three ways:

- As couples invest in each other, marriages are enriched, and that foundational block of community—the family—is strengthened.
- As church couples reach out to each other and to unchurched neighbors, community is built as relationships form and deepen.
- As the church serves the larger community, there's a ripple effect—people take note of churches that meet real needs.

CHAPTER ELEVEN

IMPLEMENTATION

GETTING STARTED

So how do you launch your own date night program? Where do you get started? What's the first step?

Here are some lessons learned by Second Baptist—and some pitfalls to avoid.

DON'T OVERSTRETCH

"We had to scale the program back," Linda admits. You can avoid that problem by carefully considering the logistics before you post a sign-up sheet.

You'll be tempted to host a date night monthly. After all, couples should be going out together at least once a month, right? So why not meet the need that often?

Lots of reasons. For starters, it's likely the church calendar is already booked on some Friday nights. And it's *certainly* true that if you're relying on volunteer child care workers, they're booked most Friday evenings.

It's better to start off small and then grow the program rather than jump in and have to cancel some Fridays.

That's something that's up for discussion, too: Is Friday really the best night for your program?

DECIDE WHAT YOU'LL DO WITH THE KIDS

At Second Baptist kids enjoy a playtime, craft time, and a lesson—all the elements you'd expect to find in a Christian education environment. "The kids have to have a good time, too, or the parents won't come back," Linda says.

> **WE USUALLY GO TO DINNER AND THEN STROLL THROUGH THE MALL. IT'S A RELIEF TO BE TOGETHER AND KNOW THAT OUR SON IS IN CAPABLE, CHRISTIAN HANDS.**
> —ANISSA LAY

For a date night to work, you'll need to provide child care for at least three hours. That's what it takes to catch a movie and grab a cup of coffee or enjoy a relaxed meal.

Slapping in an old *VeggieTales* video (or two...or three) isn't providing an excellent program that will make the best use of your time with these children. It's not that Larry and Bob are terrible baby sitters...but is baby-sitting the best you can do for the children in your care?

Prepare as carefully for date night as you'd prepare any other children's ministry program. If you're not able to get new curriculum, consider recycling past vacation Bible school sessions, or recycle your favorite Sunday school sessions.

CONTROL ATTENDANCE

At Second Baptist, couples are allowed to make reservations a month in advance—but not sooner. That keeps the roster from filling up a year in advance with people who might not even be living in the area when the date night rolls around. And reservations are cut off a week before the event so organizers can be certain they have enough—but not too many—child care workers reserved for the occasion.

COUNT THE COST

Do the math carefully and realistically. If you'll be purchasing curriculum or lesson books, estimate the total cost of that resource. Add snacks, paying a staff (if you choose to do so), and any other expenses. The total may be more than you anticipated and require that you charge a fee for child care.

Before you wince, remember that parents who use the child care service expect to pay something for the privilege. That the "baby-sitting" is so inexpensive is a blessing in itself, and few parents will begrudge paying $10 for tucking multiple children into a three-hour program.

It's a bargain.

Also, you'll discover that people value something about as much as it costs to participate in it. If there's even a modest financial cost involved in reserving a space for children, parents will tend to use the service. Especially if you're unable to accommodate every parent, it's important that no-shows be kept to a minimum.

COLLECT INFORMATION

Keep the same standards in place on date nights that you'd apply to Sunday morning. Screen your volunteers. Observe the same policies your Christian education program adheres to other times children are in your facility. Know about food allergies and how to reach parents, and have a plan if a tornado alert sounds.

In short, take the child care you provide on date nights seriously.

EIGHT EASY WAYS TO ADAPT THIS IDEA

Don't assume that providing child care so parents can leave the building is the *only* way to support young families who need date nights.

Some churches, such as Saddleback Church in Lake Forest, California, host events at the church that couples can enjoy together. Sometimes those churches include child care, and sometimes they don't. It's up to you to determine what will best meet the needs of the couples in your church.

If you decide to host events but don't have the budget to hire a comedian or screen a film, here are some ideas to spark your creativity:

- **Wedding photo album table talk**—Combine a simple meal with the opportunity for couples to pass around each other's wedding photos. Encourage couples to tell the funny stories they remember from their weddings.

- **Game night**—Pull out classic board games or decks of cards. The caveat: Couples have to play as a team, and no one keeps score.
- **Park hike**—The goal is to let couples stroll hand in hand, not to scale a mountain peak. Pick a park or quiet neighborhood, and hand couples discussion starters to explore as they enjoy a leisurely walk.
- **Fondue night**—Fire up some fondue pots, and let couples move from table to table, enjoying fondue treats. Your church can provide the tidbits, or you can organize donations from participants.
- **Campfire night**—OK, maybe singing *all* the old songs is a bit much, but making s'mores is right on target. Challenge participants to tell camp stories they remember from their youth.
- **Picnic night**—Lay quilts and other blankets on the grass or on the floor, and let couples stretch out and enjoy a picnic together.
- **Star light, star bright night**—Assuming you can *see* stars from your location, ask someone who knows where to find the North Star and Jupiter to point out major constellations as couples enjoy the night air.
- **Come as you were night**—Ask couples to dress the way they dressed when they were seniors in high school. Request that high school yearbooks be brought along and shared.

FINAL THOUGHTS ABOUT...HEALTHY MARRIAGES AND YOUR CHURCH

In the end, community comes in several sizes. There's the churchwide community that shows up on Sunday morning, and there's the community of individual families.

The first can't be healthy if the second is suffering.

When your church hosts a date night program, it provides more than child care. It provides the opportunity for stressed couples to relax and remember why they fell in love in the first place. It gives them time and space to focus on each other and to celebrate their marriages.

It's a gift that will pay tremendous dividends as couples find their marriages strengthened and their commitments renewed.

> "A SUCCESSFUL MARRIAGE IS AN EDIFICE
> THAT MUST BE REBUILT EVERY DAY."
> —ANDRÉ MAUROIS

BUILD COMMUNITY AMONG WOMEN

This Bible study has thrived for more than 25 years by bringing women from many churches together and meeting their need for fellowship with other Christian women.

☑ WORKS FOR CHURCHES OF ANY SIZE

☑ BUILDS WOMEN'S MINISTRY

☑ INCLUDES BOTH LARGE- AND SMALL-GROUP COMPONENTS

☑ REQUIRES SUBSTANTIAL VOLUNTEER MANAGEMENT AND INVOLVEMENT

WELCOME

Visit the weekly women's Bible study at Faith Evangelical Church in Loveland, Colorado, and you'll find a room packed with women. Young and old, new to the study or celebrating 20 years of attendance, they all find seats after chatting and laughing awhile over cups of tea or coffee.

They've all come to the same meeting, but some have come for dramatically different reasons.

The woman there in the third row is Sheila.*

When she and John were first married, she thought she'd set sail on her lifelong dream of having a husband as excited about serving God as she is. But after the kids came and her husband's business took off, he found more and more reasons to skip a Sunday here and there. Before long they were attending church as a family only on holidays—and sometimes not even then. Sheila's come because she craves the friendship of other women who understand her situation and who will pray for her husband.

And there in the back is Nancy.* She is nearly 55, and her children have grown wings and soared from the nest. The youngest is away at college; the rest have launched careers that have taken them far away.

Nancy was wondering what purpose she had in life after dedicating nearly three decades to mothering when she realized that the church was full of young mothers who needed her. She's become a surrogate mother for some of the new moms who wonder how to handle the demands of child rearing. She's quick with a knowing nod and sometimes offers advice. But mostly Nancy provides a sympathetic, listening ear to women who are exhausted from long nights with colicky babies or demanding preschoolers. When the meeting ends, she'll be surrounded by moms with young children.

And then there's Karri.* She's perched right up front and center, her notebook open and pen in hand as a speaker begins teaching from the Bible. Karri is a spiritual sponge, always wanting to soak in more of God's Word.

Karri appreciates the friendships she's made at Women in the Word, but there's no question about it: It's the "in the Word" part of the study that keeps her coming week after week.

The names of some women have been changed to protect confidentiality.

Sheila, Nancy, and Karri came through the door hoping for three dramatically different payoffs. Sheila wanted support and understanding. Nancy needed a purpose. And Karri was hunting for deep Bible study.

They all got what they needed in one place: Women in the Word. And while that's impressive, what makes it even more so is that none of the three women are actually members of Faith Evangelical.

A COMMUNITYWIDE WOMEN'S MINISTRY

In 1979, several women from Loveland were happy to have found a Bible study they all enjoyed. The teaching was solid, and the community that had formed was warm and supportive.

The only problem was location. It was a 20-mile drive to the weekly study, and that distance made it nearly impossible for many women to attend. Driving during Colorado winters was especially challenging.

So Barb Jacobson and her friends decided to start their *own* study, at their *own* church. But rather than inviting just the women in their congregation, Barb and her team were determined to make it a communitywide event.

Women could come whether or not they belonged to Barb's church. And to ensure that the study didn't become a "for our people only" program, Barb and her team invited friends from other churches. They sent announcements to other congregations. They posted fliers at local Christian bookstores. They had the study announced on a Christian radio station.

"My hairdresser even put up a poster," says Barb.

No one remembers how many women attended the first meeting, but they weren't all from Faith Evangelical. Nor were they the same age. What they had in common was a desire to study God's Word.

And in joining together to fulfill that desire, they created a community.

The study has been well attended for more than 25 years. "Right now we have 134 women registered," says Barb, who reports that through the years attendance has ranged between 100 and 150.

But attendance is just part of the story. Women in the Word has been successful in other ways, too.

BIBLE STUDY AS A FRIENDSHIP INCUBATOR

Because from its inception Women in the Word has included a small-group component, some participants have been friends for years. "We're intentional about creating discussion groups that mix younger and older women," says Barb. "One of our older members is 85 this year, and we've got women who are in their 20s."

Small groups have become "friendship incubators," places where women launch and build relationships. It's a happy coincidence of sorts; the small groups were originally conceived as opportunities to apply the Bible teaching to daily life. And while that's happening, the groups have become important in themselves, apart from the teaching.

"We're studying Romans this year," says Tricia Coffey, who recently began attending Women in the Word. "I went to Bible college, and I've read Romans many times. I don't expect to hear much I haven't heard before. But I enjoy being with these women. We're becoming friends."

In a world in which frequent relocations and changing marital status often set women afloat in new locations, the chance to make new friends is a huge benefit. That benefit hasn't been lost on the leaders of Women in the Word, who encourage friendships to deepen by assigning women to small groups and then keeping the groups consistent throughout the year.

BUILDING ON A COMMON FOUNDATION

It would be a mistake to consider Women in the Word a social club. It isn't. From its beginning, the group's leadership has kept a laser-like focus on Bible study. "We've kept Bible study our focus because it's vital," says Barb Jacobson. "And the studies give us a common foundation."

That focus and common foundation are reflected in how meetings are structured. Women in the Word meets Thursday mornings from 9:00 to 11:00; here's a typical agenda:

8:00 a.m.—Designated group members arrive to ensure the meeting space is set up properly (classrooms for small-group use and rows of chairs in the multipurpose room for large-group teaching). Other group members fire up the coffee pots and prepare the tea. Still others set out blank name tags and markers.

8:45 to 9:00 a.m.—The large room echoes with laughter and conversation as women greet each other and collect cups of coffee and tea.

9:00 to 9:15 a.m.—Small groups of women gather in classrooms off the larger room. Each group opens with prayer requests and the chance to report how past prayers have been answered.

9:15 to 10:10 a.m.—Each week, small-group members receive questions to answer before the following meeting. The questions are designed to get women thinking about what's coming in the Bible study teaching time and help group members apply the Bible truths they'll consider. Between 9:15 and 10:10, women compare their answers, discussing what they discovered about the Bible truths and themselves.

10:20 a.m.—As small groups wrap up, women drift into the larger room. After a hymn and a prayer, a speaker—a woman—opens the Bible and teaches.

11:00 a.m.—Women are dismissed, though many linger awhile to connect with one another.

> **WE ASK THE PASTOR TO TEACH ONCE TOWARD THE BEGINNING OF EACH YEAR. IT'S GOOD FOR THE WOMEN TO KNOW WHO OUR PASTOR IS.**
> —BARB JACOBSON

Note the emphasis on Bible study. The 40-minute teachings are in-depth studies, carefully prepared by one of the leaders. During a given year, four or five women share teaching responsibilities, and they take preparation seriously.

"The teacher for the coming week and the small-group leaders get together on Tuesday afternoons," says Barb. "The teacher outlines what she'll cover, and we talk through the questions that will be shared in the small groups on Thursday. We want to be certain we're prepared."

That preparation is far from casual. Teachers are assigned sections of Scripture to teach months in advance, and they're expected to craft discussion questions that help participants connect the Scripture passage to daily life up to eight *months* in advance.

"When people sign up to teach, they're making quite a commitment," says Barb in something of a classic understatement.

MAKING SMALL GROUPS WORK

While Women in the Word has kept Bible study central, there's no denying the importance of the small groups as well. That's why the leadership of Women in the Word has worked as hard to make the small-group experience as excellent as the teaching.

They have developed the following 13 expectations for how the small groups will operate and how participants will relate to each other while in the small groups.

1. The Bible is the sole authority upon which we stand and will be regarded as such.

2. Participants will prepare for small-group time by having their weekly questions answered and ready for sharing.

3. Participants will respect each other's beliefs and insights.

4. Small-group meetings will begin on schedule, so please be prompt.

5. Everyone is encouraged to participate in the discussion.

6. Cell phones will be turned off during small-group time or at least set to vibrate rather than ring.

7. Prayer requests will be concise and precise.

8. Prayer requests will be presented in a tasteful manner.

9. What is shared in your small group will be kept in confidence. Nothing you hear is to be repeated outside the group.

10. Generosity in your donations and time is vital and appreciated.

11. Small groups will not be used as an opportunity to advance business opportunities or make specialized announcements.

12. Tapes of the teachings are available to check out or to buy. If you miss a weekly teaching, you're expected to review it promptly.

13. You're expected to learn, grow, share, and have fun!

THE IMPORTANCE OF CHILD CARE

If you want young women to attend any event, you can't overestimate the importance of providing excellent child care.

"For the first few years, we had a playroom for children," remembers Barb Jacobson. "Then it dawned on us that if we were going to have children for several hours a week, we should be doing more than baby-sitting. We should be *teaching* the children something."

The leadership team quickly created a nursery and classes for two age groups: 2- and 3-year-olds, and 4- and 5-year-olds. Older children don't come with their mothers because Women in the Word meets only when school is in session.

"At first our teachers were volunteers," says Barb. "Now we pay a stipend to our teachers. And we use a curriculum."

The child care component of Women in the Word is funded by weekly donations given by women who use the child care service as well as some who don't. There's no set amount for donations, as the leadership team never wants financial constraints to prevent a woman from attending.

> **WE SPEND LOTS OF TIME PRAYING ABOUT WHAT PASSAGE TO STUDY THE NEXT YEAR. IT'S A KEY DECISION FOR LEADERSHIP TO MAKE FROM YEAR TO YEAR.**
> —BARB JACOBSON

PLANNING AN ANNUAL CALENDAR

Because Women in the Word aims for large attendance and a well-organized Bible study, the effort requires planning. *Lots* of planning. Lots of planning *and* several months of preparation.

The weekly Bible studies begin in mid-September and wrap up with a brunch in mid-May. But experience has shown that pulling together those eight months of programming is a year-around effort. The following annual calendar lists major tasks:

May—Following the brunch concluding the year's meetings, the leaders of Women in the Word meet to evaluate the year that just ended. Did the teachings meet the needs of participants? Was the feedback positive? What book of the Bible would speak to the women likely to attend during the upcoming year? There's a great deal of prayer and discussion, as well as crossing items off a to-do list.

Thank you notes are written to those who stepped forward to serve the previous year. Bible study teachers are recruited and scheduled for the following year. The local school district is contacted to determine what Thursdays will fall during spring break, graduations, and other school events.

June—Leaders recruit small-group leaders and volunteers to organize coffee and tea, the sound system, and table decorations. Leaders work with speakers to determine which sections of Scripture will be covered on which weeks. Speakers are coached on how to write open-ended, compelling questions about their Scripture passages. The questions are collected in a handbook that is given to each participant at the first meeting in September. About a dozen questions are expected for each weekly meeting.

July—Publicity is planned for the coming year. Bulletin announcements appear in local congregations.

August—Publicity efforts intensify as letters are mailed to past participants announcing the date of the September kick-off meeting. The handbook of questions is proofread and printed. The leadership team, small-group leaders, and speakers meet in the middle of the month to finalize details. At this meeting, attendees make room signs for the different small groups; plan for food, coffee, flowers, and table numbers; decide how to distribute publicity fliers to area churches, Christian bookstores, and Christian radio stations; and write an ad to be placed in the local newspaper.

September—Ads appear in the paper, and the town is blanketed with fliers. The handbook is ready, and the sound committee is trained. Before the first meeting, room signs are hung, and the children's director is recruited to coordinate child care details. The church custodian and church property committee are given set-up directions.

The first meeting is held in mid-September, and meetings are held weekly through mid-May. Exceptions are made on Thursdays when the local schools aren't in session.

October—A directory of participants is assembled, including each registered participant's name and phone number. Logistical problems are identified. Are coffee and tea available? Any concerns from the church custodian? Are the teachers delivering meaty, relevant teaching? Are small groups becoming cohesive? If challenges are identified, they're evaluated now, early in the year. Also in October, a Christmas brunch is planned.

November—Details of the Christmas brunch are finalized. Each participant is encouraged to invite a woman who might be interested in Women in the Word.

December—The Christmas brunch is pulled together by volunteer committees who handle invitations, food, decorations, and entertainment (typically a musical group). Leaders send volunteers thank you notes.

January—Meetings resume following the New Year's holiday, after school begins.

February—Planning begins for the spring brunch.

March—At Thursday meetings the topic for the following year is announced. The topic might be a book of the Bible or a collection of books of the Bible such as selected letters of Paul.

April—Advertising begins for the mid-May brunch, which is organized by committees similar to those that organized the Christmas brunch. Evaluations are prepared to distribute at the brunch.

"It's absolutely worth the effort to do all the planning so far in advance," says Barb Jacobson. "Then the rest of the year is much easier."

C H A P T E R　　T W E L V E
IMPLEMENTATION

GETTING STARTED

Want to launch a communitywide, community-building women's Bible study of your own? Here's some advice based on the experience of Women in the Word.

VERIFY THE VISION

Opening up the study to women who aren't part of your faith tradition means you have to focus on what you have in common, not denominational distinctives. It also means your "home team" may be uncomfortable from time to time. If your church is a "hand-raising" church during worship, how will you feel when women from other backgrounds steadfastly refuse to do so? Or vice versa? Expect some unexpected cultural conflicts.

CRANK UP THE ADVERTISING

It's far easier to invite your own people than to reach women from other churches, but you won't have a communitywide program if only your own church members participate. Advertise widely but carefully: *You* know you're simply inviting other women to a Bible-based study. Other churches might wonder if you're trolling for new church members.

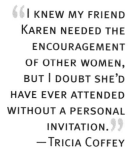

> "I KNEW MY FRIEND KAREN NEEDED THE ENCOURAGEMENT OF OTHER WOMEN, BUT I DOUBT SHE'D HAVE EVER ATTENDED WITHOUT A PERSONAL INVITATION."
> —TRICIA COFFEY

The safest advertising is the most personal: Encourage your existing members to invite friends. "Word of mouth is what really gets the job done," says Barb Jacobson. "When friends invite friends, people come."

REALIZE YOU CAN'T SERVE EVERY WOMAN

The Thursday morning meeting time effectively eliminates many working women. Some are able to schedule around meeting days; most can't.

"We picked a time that works for many women, but we know not everyone who'd like to come can make it," says Barb Jacobson.

But what day and time *would* work for everyone?

Do some homework so you know what other Bible study and small-group options exist in your church and other faithful churches. You'll be able to refer women who can't make it to your Bible study to others.

EMBRACE TEAMWORK

It's clear that this kind of effort requires a team to organize and implement it. A project this size requires that you first build a team to share decision-making and tasks.

FINAL THOUGHTS ABOUT...CREATING YOUR OWN BIBLE STUDY FOR WOMEN

Excellent resources already exist for women's Bible studies. Some are provided by organizations like Bible Study Fellowship International; others, such as *Experiencing God* by Henry Blackaby and Claude V. King, are classics. Still others—dozens—are written by leading women teachers such as Beth Moore, Kay Arthur, Joni Eareckson Tada, and Anne Graham Lotz.

With so many studies already in existence, why should your church bother to write its own?

Here are two reasons worth considering:

First, selecting the Bible passage allows your leadership to pinpoint the most important, relevant passage for the specific women taking part in the study. You know your situation and the women you serve better than anyone else.

Second, creating lessons requires a hefty investment of time and energy. This kind of investment engenders a deep sense of ownership that will contribute to the study's long-term success.

Whether you develop your own study or use one developed by someone else, use women's Bible studies to build community among the women who attend. This intentional focus will generate and nurture friendships for years to come, creating ever-increasing accountability and discipleship opportunities.

"CHARM IS DECEPTIVE, AND BEAUTY IS FLEETING;
BUT A WOMAN WHO FEARS THE LORD IS TO BE PRAISED."
—PROVERBS 31:30

BUILD COMMUNITY AMONG MOTHERS OF YOUNG CHILDREN

This church connects moms of young children while giving them a break from their stressful lives.

☑ WORKS WELL IN CHURCHES WITH YOUNG FAMILIES

☑ WORKS FOR CHURCHES OF ANY SIZE

☑ DEEPENS AND EXPANDS SMALL-GROUP MINISTRIES

GIVING MOMS A BREAK

Mothers of young children are often exhausted, exasperated, and lonely. Because young children require constant attention, moms rarely have time for themselves. Many find themselves without friends, desperate for interaction with other adults. They long to connect with other women who understand their situation and can offer spiritual and emotional sustenance.

In 2000, some of the stay-at-home moms at Woodland Hills Church in St. Paul, Minnesota, formed a weekly gathering called Mom's Together Loving Children. In the early stages of this ministry, the women looked for ways to get together through play dates, picnics, and other opportunities to get out of the house with the kids—crucial during long winter months in the upper Midwest.

During this time, the church had been meeting in rented school facilities. When the church completed its building, Lea Wilson had a vision for expanding this ministry beyond social connections. As she talked with the other moms and Lyn Foote, a pastor on staff, a new ministry was born: the Spiritual Spa.

SPIRITUAL REFRESHMENT

The ministry's mission is "to encourage and spiritually empower each other as a community of mothers with young children to minister to our families, the church, and beyond as the Lord leads." The aim is to create a space and time for women to refresh their souls. Rather than parenting strategies or specific child-related issues, spiritual refreshment is the focus.

The Spa was an immediate hit among mothers of young children. Since its inception in 2002, 65 to 70 women have gathered each Thursday morning at the church to minister to one another. In the process, a very special community has formed.

WHAT IT HAS REALLY MEANT

Today, the Spiritual Spa is one of the most effective ministries in the church. Jill Krummen, a mother of two, says the weekly fellowship has "helped me feel connected and has given me an opportunity to have meaningful relationships with other Christian moms."

Bethany Peterson, a new mother, agrees, adding, "The Spa has helped me prioritize my life."

Patty Carey has seven children, ranging from just under 10 months to 10 years of age. She says, "Listening to other moms motivates me. Talking to them and learning how they parent has really helped me."

Rachel Scott has been a member since the Spa's inception, has two young boys, and leads worship during the large-group session. She says, "The Spa has challenged me to become a more conscientious parent and has made me much more aware of my kids' spiritual development and needs."

Another member says, "Being a mother can be all-consuming, but it's not the only role we play. We all long to be deeply connected to our spouses. Many of us work at least part-time, which complicates our lives even more. At the Spa, we openly share how hard all of this can be in the midst of raising small children. The Spa validates us as we try to balance all of our roles."

The ministry's impact is felt throughout the church. A husband of one of the leaders has noticed that these women connect with one another on a deeper, more consistent level than members of most of the other small groups in the church.

EVERY THURSDAY MORNING

Show up at Woodland Hills Church on a Thursday morning during the school year, and you'll find a parking lot full of young mothers pushing strollers and leading toddlers by the hand, as they join other moms—friends, now—for a morning of laughter, sharing, and sometimes tears.

The women gather from 9:30 to 11:15 a.m. Here is a typical agenda:

9:15 to 9:30—Drop off children
9:30 to 9:40—Welcome and announcements
9:40 to 10:15—Corporate worship
10:15 to 11:15—Small group discussion
11:15—Pick up children

INTENTIONAL COMMUNITY BUILDING

It is typical for women's ministries to gather in a large group and then form small groups for discussion. But the Spa has been built upon a slightly different vision—a vision emphasizing community, not programmatic ministry.

As a result, the small groups that meet after corporate worship are composed of women who meet with one another every week. Over time, they've attained a degree of intimacy and trust that isn't possible in randomly formed groups.

These groups are part of the church's larger vision for community and are called covenant groups. According to the church's Web site (www.whchurch.org), "At Woodland Hills, Covenant Groups are the primary community where our church vision becomes reality. As we know and are known, bless and are blessed, we advance the Kingdom of God against the kingdom of darkness as a mighty, unified army."

The church offers two sessions each year: one in the spring and one in the fall. Six to eight groups meet during each session. According to Lyn Foote, who leads this ministry, these groups help individualistic Americans experience community on an entry level. Lyn's greater hope is that the relationships formed in the Spa will naturally flow into other areas of the participants' lives. Many have.

BEYOND THURSDAY MORNINGS

Spa participants often connect over coffee during the week or gather for a moms' night out. One mother says, "I moved to St. Paul tired and a bit burned out by previous church experiences. But now I've found a place where I can be myself with women who will love me in the midst of life."

Since the Spa's beginning, four small groups that have "graduated" (their children have all entered school) have begun meeting at other times during the week. Another group has evolved into a couples' group, as the wives invited their husbands to join them for weekly get-togethers.

This couples' group has become a community in the best sense of the word. Recently, the men in the group gathered to put a new roof on the home of one of the couples. The leader, Patrick, fell off the roof and broke his back. The members rallied around Patrick and his wife, Lynette, to support them in extraordinary ways.

For example, the group cared for Patrick and Lynette's three little girls, one of whom was less than a month old when Patrick had his accident. In addition, the group provided a steady supply of meals and groceries. The group sacrificed for months, consistently providing for the family in practical ways over the long term. And it all began with the community that formed and was nurtured at the Spiritual Spa.

DIVIDE AND CONQUER

When Lea Wilson proposed the idea of the Spa, the vision grabbed her, and she embraced it wholeheartedly. As the initial director, she did everything to get the ministry off the ground. She recruited the children's workers—mostly her friends—and she planned and executed nearly every detail of the ministry.

But she and her husband lived an hour from the church and decided to attend a church closer to their home. The Spa had been in effect for just one session. At that point, the ministry could have easily withered away.

Enter Melanie Zeuske. Her gifts were different from Lea's. Realizing that she and other busy moms don't have time to take on huge jobs, she organized the ministry so that it could be accomplished by several people doing manageable tasks. Although she served as the director for only one session, her role was crucial to the ministry's long-term effectiveness.

Now several women lead the ministry's various teams. As you can see from the following descriptions, each role is significant, but none is so large that it is overwhelming.

- **Ministry Director**—Oversees all Spiritual Spa activities and is the liaison between the ministry and the church. She spends about five hours a week in this role.

- **Newsletter Coordinator**—Oversees the team that writes, produces, and mails the ministry newsletter four times a year. There are five to six members of the team; each spends one to five hours on the newsletter four times a year.

- **Registration Coordinator**—Oversees the team that registers participants. This team has three to four members. Each puts in 10 to 15 hours twice a year.

- **Event Coordinator**—Oversees the following teams:
  › **Welcoming Team**—Makes coffee and juice, sets up the welcome table and name tags, and posts necessary signs. The three to four members of this team accomplish these tasks in 15 minutes each week.
  › **Prep-for-Next-Week Team**—Stores signs and items from the refreshment and welcome tables. There are three to four people on this team, and their tasks require about 15 minutes of their time each week.
  › **Spa Brunch Team**—Organizes a brunch that is held at the end of each session. There are four to five members of this team, and each spends two to eight hours preparing for the brunch.
  › **Worship Team**—With three to five vocalists and helpers on this team, the leader plans and leads worship each week. This requires two to three hours of each member's week.
  › **Coaching Team**—This team encourages and trains small-group leaders. Each coach spends about three hours a week in this role.

- **Small-Group Leaders and Co-leaders**—Each small group has a leader who leads discussion and prayer and encourages members to extend their relationships beyond Thursday mornings. This requires five to seven hours a week. Much of this time is spent connecting with small-group members during the week and encouraging them, in turn, to connect with one another.

WHAT ABOUT THE CHILDREN?

One of the Spiritual Spa's most appealing features is the wonderful children's ministry, Jesus Junction, that the church offers to children of Spa participants. On any given Thursday, as many as 150 children come through the church doors, and the church is prepared for them. While giving tired mothers a time of fellowship with friends, the church cares for their children in a safe, nurturing environment.

During its initial session, the church asked volunteers to look after the children. But beginning with the second session, the church hired teachers and assistants to care for them. Because the Spa is held during the school year, all of the children are preschoolers and range in age from infancy to 4 years. Children are grouped according to age, and teachers use children's curricula selected by the church. Teachers are paid $25, and assistants are paid $20 each week. To provide consistency, teachers and assistants work with the same groups of children from week to week, following standard rules established by the children's ministry of the church.

Each week, a different small group looks after the babies (infants up to a year old). So, even though they're not in their traditional group setting, these women still have time to connect with one another.

JESUS JUNCTION

Woodland Hills views Jesus Junction as a parallel ministry to the Spiritual Spa and has hired a coordinator to oversee it. This releases the Spa's director to focus on moms because she is confident that the children are being cared for with the same intentionality and focus.

Here are the roles of the people caring for the children:

- **Coordinator**—Oversees all aspects of the Jesus Junction ministry, including recruiting and supervising teachers. These responsibilities take about eight hours a week.
- **Activities Team**—Prior to each bi-annual session of the Spiritual Spa, this team of two to three selects and organizes the activities that children between the ages of 2 and 5 will take part in throughout the session. Each team member spends about 10 planning hours before each session.
- **Teachers and Assistants**—Interact with and minister to the children attending Jesus Junction. This requires about two hours every Thursday morning.
- **Snack Team**—The two to three members of this team place snacks in individual cups for 60 to 70 children and set out water pitchers and cups each Thursday morning. This takes about 20 minutes.

- **Closing-Down-the-Party Team**—The five to six members of this team spray disinfectant on toys and tables and tidy the children's classrooms at the conclusion of each Jesus Junction. This takes about 15 minutes each week.

FUNDING

Because the Spiritual Spa is self-sustaining and not a part of the church's budgeted ministries, each woman pays a $50 fee for each bi-annual session. The fee is the same regardless of the number of children each woman brings. The fees pay for all of the Jesus Junction teachers as well as scholarships for moms who cannot afford the fee. There may be an additional cost if participants are asked to purchase a book or other study materials during the course of the session.

The money is handled through the church's bookkeeping system. All of the fees are processed through the church, and the church pays all the expenses out of those fees. This keeps things simple and limits the temptations that go with handling lots of money.

CHAPTER THIRTEEN
IMPLEMENTATION

STARTING A SPIRITUAL SPA

If this idea resonates with you and your church, consider taking the following steps.

1. **Get in touch with your demographic.** Who is this ministry targeting? What are the specific needs of this group? How many existing church members fit within this group?

2. **Write a statement of purpose.** What boundaries will guide this ministry? What are the non-negotiable foundations of the vision?

3. **Identify a director.** This person must possess a heartfelt vision for this ministry as well as a real passion for helping mothers of young children.

4. **Build a team.** Make sure that most of the team members are within the demographic you've targeted. In other words, if your target is moms of young children, don't recruit team leaders who are primarily moms of grown children.

5. **Recruit and train small-group leaders.** Apply the same standards that your church uses in recruiting and training its other small-group leaders.

6. **Coach the leaders.** Don't overlook the vital role of a coach of the small-group leaders. Without a coach, group leaders will lose vision and focus.

7. **Cast the vision again and again.** Lyn says, "This is a volunteer-driven ministry. And because the volunteers naturally graduate from this ministry as their children grow older, there is a high turnover of leaders. It therefore requires lots and lots of vision casting to maintain quality leadership.

"Each year, I guide the team to focus on the central vision of building community through small groups. If small-group leaders lose that vision, they will create more and more activities that compete with our vision for developing relationships.

"These activities are not bad in themselves, but when added to the basic elements that are already in place, they would result in administrative overload for this group of volunteers."

HeartSpa™

Take your ministry to moms of young children one step further by offering them a weekend retreat. Check out HeartSpa™ (Group Publishing, 2005), a women's retreat designed to help women grow in genuine relationships, faith, and outreach.

FINAL THOUGHTS ABOUT...LONG-TERM EFFECTIVENESS

To sustain this ministry, current leaders must constantly think about those whom God is developing to serve as future leaders. If the experience of Woodland Hills Church is any indication, this ministry will draw more and more participants each year. But, without trained, qualified small-group leaders, the ministry will begin to lose its efficacy. To be effective, small groups shouldn't include more than 10 people; whenever a group is larger than this, the level of transparency greatly diminishes. The single most important step you can take to ensure the long-term success of your ministry to mothers of young children is to continually identify and train qualified small-group leaders.

> "SO IMMENSE ARE THE CLAIMS ON A MOTHER, PHYSICAL CLAIMS ON HER BODILY AND BRAIN VIGOR, AND MORAL CLAIMS ON HER HEART AND THOUGHT, THAT SHE CANNOT...MEET THEM ALL AND FIND ANY LARGE MARGIN BEYOND FOR OTHER CARES AND WORK."
>
> —FRANCES POWER COBBE

BUILD COMMUNITY THROUGH SIX-WEEK SPIRITUAL ADVENTURES

Twice a year, this church focuses all of its efforts on one spiritual theme, uniting its people around a common purpose while extending and deepening their connections to one another.

- ☑ INTEGRATES SUNDAY SERMONS WITH SMALL GROUPS AND PERSONAL DEVOTIONS
- ☑ PROMOTES SMALL GROUPS
- ☑ REQUIRES A SHORT-TERM COMMITMENT TO SMALL GROUPS
- ☑ INCLUDES BOTH LARGE- AND SMALL-GROUP COMPONENTS
- ☑ WORKS FOR CHURCHES OF ANY SIZE

THE IMPORTANCE OF FOCUS

During a regular church attender's typical week, he or she is exposed to many different biblical texts and topics. The preacher gives a sermon on one topic; a small group discusses another; personal devotions delve into a different theme each day; women's and men's meetings address still others. It's not unusual for the average church attender to catch a smattering of four or five different biblical themes during a week. This allows an individual to just skim the surface of the truth of each theme, leaving little time for life application or personal transformation.

The Vineyard Church in Champaign, Illinois, has changed this pattern. For six weeks each fall and spring, the church concentrates on one theme, not only during Sunday worship services but also during small-group sessions, personal devotions, and big events sponsored by the church.

Members of church leadership began this pattern in the fall of 2003 when they wrote a six-week series entitled "Doing the Stuff." In this series they addressed the core values of the church with the aim of inviting people into a higher level of commitment to the church's vision and calling. Since then, they have led the church through what they call a spiritual campaign or a spiritual adventure twice each year. All of the church leaders value these adventures so highly that they pray about the content of each one months beforehand and build their annual church calendar around them.

THE DIVIDENDS

These campaigns produce results. During one adventure, one small-group member shared with her group, "My life has been changed more in the last month than at any other time in my life."

Jim Egli, the Vineyard's small-group pastor, relates that his uncle, who lives 800 miles away in a retirement home, asked how he, too, could experience the adventure. He had heard of the spiritual adventure's impact from another pastor who adopted the pattern developed at the Vineyard. This pastor had reported that many physical healings had resulted from his congregation's six-week experience, and Jim's uncle wanted to get in on them!

Another example of the impact of the adventures is a small church plant in Atlanta. The pastor asked his people to describe on index cards what God was doing in their lives during that church's six-week campaign. Then he asked them to post the notes on a wall of the church. The wall was entirely covered with examples of how God had taught and changed them.

Dorothy Carlson, who attends the Vineyard in Champaign, confesses, "If the church had not undertaken the adventure when it did, I would not have changed my life." In the summer of 2004, she found herself rejected by her husband of 20 years, looking back at a life of disappointment and pain. She was a new Christian when she began the six-week adventure. Through her small-group experience, she discovered that other Christians experience hard times and that she doesn't have to face life's challenges alone. This experience turned her life around. Now many of her family members attend church, including some who were part of a Harley riding club with her, the Iron Horse Angels. She co-leads this group of 20 to 30 riders, and many have followed her into a life following Christ.

SIX WEEKS OF INTENSE SCRUTINY

Jim Egli has interviewed more than 50 church leaders whose churches provide six-week spiritual adventures, and every one of them considers the events positive, life-changing experiences. What makes these six-week spiritual adventures so powerful? What differentiates them from six-week sermon series, a pattern churches have been using for years? The key is that they use a variety of church events and programs to focus on a single theme, allowing them to synergistically unify the body and build community. The Champaign Vineyard uses four major opportunities to do this:

- **Sermons**—The adventure includes seven weekend sermons. The first sermon launches the adventure, and the last concludes it. All of these sermons concentrate on a different aspect of the same topic.

Here are some great topics for a six-week spiritual adventure:
- *experiencing spiritual breakthroughs*
- *following Jesus to the cross*
- *finding hope in a chaotic world*
- *living a connected life*
- *finding purpose in life*

- **Small Groups**—During the six weeks between the first and last sermons, all of the church's small groups are invited to participate in this adventure through the use of study guides delving into the same topic. Many churches encourage their small groups to discuss the Bible text from the weekly Sunday sermon.

- **Daily Devotions**—This element substantially deepens the impact of the spiritual adventure. Adventurers wrestle with the same topic on a more personal level as they read a devotional or another book. Devotionals are especially good at breaking down comprehensive themes into bite-size pieces.

- **Big Events**—The Vineyard tops off each spiritual adventure with a big event designed to reinforce the theme and move people forward in discipleship and equipping others. These events might come in the form of a retreat, a seminar, or special training. For example, during the adventure focusing on its vision and values, the church offered a training session entitled "Learning to Minister Like Jesus." At the conclusion of an adventure that concentrated on overcoming the sources of perpetual sin, the church held a seminar called "God, Men, and Sex." At this writing, the church is planning an adventure called "Naturally Supernatural." At its conclusion, the people will be encouraged to take part in a special "Holy Spirit Day," the goal of which will be to help them personally experience the Holy Spirit in an initial or deeper way.

RIPPLE EFFECTS

Asking for a commitment of only six weeks makes it much easier to recruit both small-group leaders and members. Spiritual adventures are therefore great places to start new groups with up-and-coming leaders. And while a six-week commitment may seem paltry to many seasoned churchgoers, people new to the church and the claims of Christ are much more likely to join a small group if they know they aren't committed indefinitely.

The strategy has worked: Each time the Champaign Vineyard completes a spiritual adventure, new groups continue to meet on a permanent basis, and people new to established groups remain in them.

LESSONS LEARNED

Over the past 25 years, Jim Egli has fine-tuned his approach to developing and implementing six-week spiritual adventures and offers these keys to success:

- Talk to other leaders whose churches have embarked on spiritual adventures to learn from their enthusiasm, success, and mistakes.
- Pray about the topic or theme of the spiritual adventure. This is not about using the hottest new material. It's about accelerating what you've discerned that God wants to do *in your church at this time.*
- Plan far in advance, especially if you are writing your own material.

Select a theme at least six months before launching the adventure.

- Dovetail training of small-group leaders with the launch of the event. Recruit leaders, train them, and then launch the new groups.
- Incorporate into your adventures events that mobilize people in ministry and outreach,

CHAPTER FOURTEEN
IMPLEMENTATION

PREPARATION FOR
THE ADVENTURE

After years of refining spiritual adventures, Jim Egli has found that the most important key to success is careful preparation. The preparation isn't complex, but it does require forethought and intentionality. Here are the steps to take:

1. **Seek God's leading in your choice of a topic.** Every congregation is unique and faces a specific set of circumstances and challenges. Ask God to show you how best to address your church's unique needs through a six-week campaign.

2. **Set dates for the adventure.** Jim has found the best times to be the end of September through early November, Lent, or the six weeks after Easter. Jim says, "Don't start in early September. Many people are just getting re-involved in church after school has started and need a few weeks to evaluate this opportunity."

3. **Decide on the topic at least six months before the launch date.** This lead time is absolutely necessary to properly prepare and promote a successful adventure.

4. **Recruit a volunteer director.** Give this person the responsibility of working with the point person on the pastoral staff to prepare the event. This person should be a good manager of people and schedules. This is not an up-front position, but rather a behind-the-scenes, detail-oriented role.

5. **Secure materials.** Many small-group study guides and daily devotionals are available for six-week spiritual adventures. Begin the search for appropriate materials several months before the launch date, as a thorough evaluation takes time. Or you may decide to create your own, which is even more time-consuming.

6. **Recruit new leaders.** Two months before the launch, talk with current small-group leaders about potential leaders, and talk to people you think would make good leaders. Meet with them and personally invite them to the training.

7. **Train new leaders.** Provide introductory training for leading a small group. This training need not be exhaustive, only enough to get the leader started. (Four hours of training on a Saturday is usually sufficient.) If new leaders want to continue leading groups after the adventure, provide further training at that point.

   An excellent resource for small-group leaders is *Small Group Ministry in the 21st Century* (Group Publishing, Inc., 2005). In it, leaders will find practical guidance in every aspect of small-group leadership.

8. **Promote the adventure.** Remember this principle: Half of church attenders come only half of the time. Therefore, the announcement for the upcoming adventure should be made by the senior pastor from the pulpit each of the six weeks preceding the launch. Without this kind of emphasis by the senior pastor, the people will perceive the adventure as a nice option but not an all-church effort. In addition, use bulletin announcements, Web postings, posters, and other appropriate forms of promotion.

> Don't spring a spiritual adventure on the congregation the week before the adventure starts. The fruit will be no greater than that of any other six-week sermon series.

9. **Sign up new small-group members.** During the three weeks leading up to the launch, invite people not currently in groups to sign up for them. Give them options. For example, allow them to choose a group based upon the day of the week it meets or geographical location, especially important if your church is in a large city.

10. **Sell the book of devotions you've selected or written.** Offer the books for sale during the month before the launch. This is a great way to promote the adventure. Also, if you wait until the Sunday before the launch to sell the books, 25 percent of the church will miss the opportunity.

What About Small Churches?

Twenty years ago, Jim Egli led a church of 50 on six-week spiritual adventures. They worked then the same way they work now with more than 1,000 people. All of the principles are the same.

FREQUENCY

The Vineyard in Champaign holds spiritual adventures twice a year. One begins at the end of September, and the other is held during Lent. This church has a healthy and mature small-group system, complete with ongoing training and an infrastructure of volunteer coaches and small-group pastors. If your church doesn't have this kind of established support, consider launching a spiritual adventure once a year. Evaluate the experience; then go from there.

LONG-TERM SUCCESS

Spiritual adventures can supercharge a church around a single vision and deepen and extend the congregation's sense of connectedness and community. But that sense of community will be short-lived if the church doesn't make a long-term commitment to small groups. Without support from the church in the form of small-group coaches, ongoing leadership training, and support meetings, small groups will dwindle and fade.

FINAL THOUGHTS ABOUT...UNITY THROUGH FOCUS

Jim Egli concludes, "Six-week spiritual adventures now help to define our church. Each adventure invites all of the dispersed individuals of the church to rally around a single theme. For many, this kind of unity is unprecedented. The more of these adventures we provide, the more connected our people become to one another and to the mission of the church."

"MAY THE GOD WHO GIVES ENDURANCE AND ENCOURAGEMENT GIVE YOU A SPIRIT OF UNITY AMONG YOURSELVES AS YOU FOLLOW CHRIST JESUS, SO THAT WITH ONE HEART AND MOUTH YOU MAY GLORIFY THE GOD AND FATHER OF OUR LORD JESUS CHRIST." —ROMANS 15:5-6

BUILD COMMUNITY
WITH SHUT-INS

To encourage homebound people during Advent, this church
delivers baskets packed with fruit and thoughtful gifts.

☑ WORKS FOR CHURCHES OF ANY SIZE
☑ BUILDS INTERGENERATIONAL COMMUNITY
☑ REQUIRES SIGNIFICANT SUPPLIES
☑ REQUIRES GOOD VOLUNTEER MANAGEMENT
☑ SEASONAL

REMEMBERING THE ABSENT

"Out of sight, out of mind."

No one knows who said those words first, but the *last* place you'll hear them is at Highland United Methodist Church in Raleigh, North Carolina.

At Highland United Methodist, "out of sight people" *are* remembered. And during Advent, people who aren't able to attend worship services because they're ill, who are recovering after surgery or childbirth, or who are in extended care situations are remembered in a *big* way.

Lisa Burney coordinates an annual effort to create and distribute Advent gift baskets packed with fruit and personal care items to shut-ins. The church launched the effort in 1987, and each year since the church has fine-tuned the program.

"It's become a tradition," Lisa says. "And it's a tradition I most definitely want to keep alive." She isn't the only one who feels that way.

'TIS MORE BLESSED TO GIVE THAN TO RECEIVE

Mrs. Pat Zachary, 87, received a basket during the 2005 Advent season.

Pat has slowed down a bit now that she's in her 80s, but that's been a recent development. She and her husband were traveling regularly until the November she discovered she has cancer.

"I haven't been to church in some time," she says. "I can't go, and that's been difficult. I've been a member of the church for so long."

Though church staff and friends gathered around as Pat started her course of cancer treatment, she welcomed the arrival of the fruit basket at Advent. "It was a great thing receiving that basket. It was so pretty and full of good things. Grapes, apples, bananas, tangerines—I enjoyed it."

But the real benefit to Pat wasn't the arrival of fresh fruit. Rather, it was that the basket sitting on her table reminded her that members of her church hadn't forgotten her.

Plus, the basket gave her one more reason to get healthy.

"I look forward to participating in the basket program in the future," she says, "but as someone who *gives* the baskets, not someone who receives more of them."

O'Dell Massey and his wife, Amy, have delivered Advent baskets together for several years.

"Amy is involved in lots of things at the church," O'Dell laughs. "I don't volunteer to do much, but Amy signs me up at the drop of a hat. I'm always finding out that I'm signed up to do something."

One of those "somethings" was to deliver Advent baskets. So with Amy beside him and a basket or two in the backseat, O'Dell drove off to make deliveries.

It's an experience he says he won't forget. "One of the ladies in our church is a nurse, and she knew of a home where there were three generations living together—a grandmother, her daughter, and several grandkids. The daughter had been diagnosed with breast cancer, and the family was struggling.

"They were delighted to receive a fruit basket, and truth be told—it's something they could use. One of the grandsons had never eaten an apple before."

While Amy signed O'Dell up the first time, making deliveries was something he *wanted* to do the next year—and in the future.

While delivering baskets the Masseys often are invited into peoples' homes, and they're able to strike up conversations. "We've gotten to know some remarkable people," says Massey.

People who receive gift baskets during the second week of December aren't the only ones who appreciate the Advent gift basket project. The rest of the congregation benefits as well.

> **"WE GET MORE JOY GIVING THE BASKETS THAN THE PEOPLE WHO RECEIVE THEM EXPERIENCE. NO DOUBT ABOUT IT."**
> **—O'DELL MASSEY**

"This project gets everyone in our congregation involved in missions," says Lisa Burney. "Sunday school classes close their doors on the Sunday morning we make baskets, and everyone gathers in our multipurpose area to work together."

The church refers to the Advent basket-making event as their Care and Share Festive Family Affair, a title that does a fair job describing the project, though it fails to mention one of the program's more distinctive elements.

And that would be the pancakes.

BREAKFAST IS SERVED

Nobody beats Highland's men's group at cranking out mouth-watering pancakes—and that's how the second Sunday in December always begins.

The men start cooking during the first worship service, reports Lisa, and the scent of pancakes, bacon, scrambled eggs, sausage, and grits is one of her more effective recruiting tools. "By the time the first service has ended, there's a line outside the serving station," she says. "Some people come hungry. Others get that way when they smell what's cooking."

Breakfast is a break-even affair. Donations tossed in a basket near the serving table take care of expenses, and the suggested donation is $1.

Church members eat at tables set up in the church's multipurpose room. After everyone has had a helping or two of flapjacks and eggs, tables are cleared, and volunteers from the church's family ministry team set several empty baskets on each table. At the far end of the room, more tables are heaped high with the fruit, nuts, sweets, and personal care items (lotions and soaps) that church members have brought from home that morning.

And that's when the real fun begins.

LEAVING IT UP TO THE HOLY SPIRIT

Lisa and her team ask church members to bring fresh fruit and other items to put in the gift baskets, but they don't assign specific items to specific families.

"We leave that up to the Holy Spirit," says Lisa. "We always seem to get what we need and usually end up with a bounty—more than we can use. When that happens, a church member loads up what's left and takes it to a soup kitchen so it won't be wasted."

Don't think Lisa is disorganized—that's not the case. Not only is the event well advertised and tightly scheduled, but prior to the event the pastor teaches about the rationale behind the upcoming mission project.

"We have a special lesson explaining *why* we're serving others," Lisa says. "We tie the event to the gift of Jesus. Rather than just maintaining a tradition or doing something we've always done, we're giving—because God gave to us and our giving expresses our love for God."

Lisa refuses to choreograph certain portions of the event because she's serious about keeping first things first.

"We're making baskets, but more than that we're making a community. That's why we leave it up to the Holy Spirit as to what ends up in each basket, and who ends up working together to fill the baskets."

At table after table, high school students work alongside senior citizens, families with young children figure out the best way to balance apples with bananas, and groups of people who barely know each other team up to create baskets. There's no "right" way to fill a basket, so cooperation is key.

And cooperation is exactly what happens.

The empty red and green, woven baskets are purchased at a local farmer's market and are quickly filled with a selection of fruit and other items. To keep contents fresh and in place, baskets are lined with colorful Christmas wrap, covered with clear plastic wrap, and then topped off with a felt bow. Finally a tag—decorated by children in the church and signed by everyone who helped create the basket—is carefully taped to the finished basket.

Within an hour, rows of baskets are lined up, ready to be delivered.

DELIVERY WITH A SMILE

Baskets of fresh fruit require prompt delivery, and this is another time that Lisa trusts God to arrange connections within the community of faith.

"Some people want to deliver baskets to specific shut-ins, but often it's a matter of geography—who's heading in which direction.

"And I love to see young families making deliveries. One of our families with young children moved here from the Midwest. All the children's grandparents are in Ohio, and they're able to get together at most once a year. By delivering baskets, this family has sparked a relationship with elderly people they wouldn't have met otherwise. Now it's as if the children have great-aunts and great-uncles here in North Carolina."

One significant criterion for delivering baskets is a willingness to do it quickly. Sunday afternoon is best, though a Monday morning delivery is acceptable. "The goal is for the fresh fruit to still be fresh," Lisa says.

Delivery is more than a drop-off and handshake. Though homebound people are generally at home, they aren't always available. A phone call to arrange a time for delivery assures both the gift-bringer and the gift-receiver that the hand-off will be enjoyable and include a visit.

Arranging for delivery is one part of the process that Lisa and her team do plan. The church hosts a family from the Ukraine, and though the family doesn't worship at Highland United Methodist, the family still receives a basket. The challenge with that delivery is that no one in the sponsored family speaks English.

Lisa's solution is to see that a specific church member who *can* communicate with the family makes the delivery. The goal, after all, is to build a sense of community—not just to drop off a load of fresh fruit.

> **❝LAST YEAR WE DELIVERED ABOUT 35 BASKETS—AND WE'RE ALREADY PLANNING FOR NEXT YEAR.❞**
> —LISA BURNEY

There's a smile in Lisa's voice when she explains why the Care and Share Festive Family Affair will continue to be an annual Advent project: "Our shut-ins are members of our family," she says. "We love them and care for them even though they can't be with us on Sunday mornings. They're part of our community, and this is one way we can express Jesus' love to them."

LESSONS LEARNED

The majority of the people receiving gift baskets are elderly—and preparing baskets for the elderly requires a bit of forethought. Here are some practical tips.

Use large fonts. Be sure the writing on cards attached to baskets is easy for elderly eyes to read.

Make unwrapping the basket easy. Use plastic wrap sparingly so it's easy to remove.

Call before delivering the baskets. In addition to making certain that recipients are available, the elderly often wish to prepare for the visit. When you don't welcome many guests, you want to look your best when you do receive visitors.

Make it easy for elderly recipients to contact you. If the only contact information you provide on the card or in a letter is an e-mail address, you'll frustrate seniors who have no Web access but who still wish to send a thank you note. Provide a phone number and snail-mail address, too.

CHAPTER FIFTEEN
IMPLEMENTATION

REMEMBER THIS...

Here are additional tips Lisa and her team suggest you keep in mind if you decide to launch your own Advent gift-basket program.

Keep your list of recipients current. People die, people recover from illnesses, and people move away from your area. Don't send someone to deliver a basket only to discover when the front door is opened that your intended recipient died the previous month.

"And you don't want to deliver a basket to someone who meets you at the door and wonders why he or she is receiving a basket," Lisa cautions. "Some people who were homebound do recover, and they don't appreciate your thinking they wouldn't."

Be sensitive to the condition of the recipients. Some people are on restricted diets or otherwise unable to use the food. If that's the case, forgo the basket and make a personal visit to deliver a card. The visit will be appreciated even if you show up without bananas.

Find a way for all church members who wish to be involved to participate. If they can't attend the basket-making session, they could still provide toiletries or other small gifts to include in baskets. Lisa reports that some members of her church have provided bookmarks with Christian themes.

Provide *soft* sweets—not hard candy. Large, soft mints are a favorite in Highland's baskets because in addition to being tasty, they're easy to unwrap and chew.

Provide labels with key information for your delivery people. At Highland each group that creates a basket decides who'll drop it off. But lest someone be kindhearted but directionally challenged, Lisa supplies the name and address of each recipient on a label that's easy to affix to the basket. Since many baskets are delivered as a driver is heading home from church, it's wise to have city maps available for consultation before drivers leave your church building.

Encourage nonmembers, too. If a parishioner has a neighbor or friend who's a shut-in, create a basket for that person as well. You probably can't create a basket for *every* person in the hospital or nursing home, but try to encourage shut-ins who are relationally connected to your church members.

Avoid surprises. If you tuck homemade brownies or other treats in baskets, clearly list all ingredients on wrappers. Food allergies are common—and dangerous.

FIVE EASY WAYS TO ADAPT THIS IDEA

This program helps people experience community in two ways. First, people in crisis or unfortunate situations stay connected to the larger church family. Second, tremendous community is experienced during the creation of the Advent baskets.

Here are some non-fruity approaches to experiencing both these benefits:

- **Quilting bees**—Gathering together to create quilts or blankets isn't just for frontier parties in the 1800s. Do the same as a group to create baby blankets for crisis pregnancy centers or family shelters.
- **Canned food drives**—When teams go door to door to collect donations rather than simply provide a drop-off site, there are opportunities to reach out to neighbors as well as create significant memories among team members.

- **Winter shoveling parties**—Members of a youth group in Michigan meet after each significant snowfall, pile into vans, and under cover of darkness clear the driveways and sidewalks of elderly church members. The teens knock on doors after completing jobs to let homeowners know that the snow has been removed. The goal is to communicate God's love in a practical way, with a secondary goal of getting back to the church without getting vans stuck in snow banks!

- **Hospital visitation teams**—Not everyone in the hospital receives visitors on a regular basis. When church members or their friends are hospitalized, it's often a blessing to receive brief visits offering prayer and support. It's equally helpful for families waiting for surgery results to have a caring team at their side.

- **Listening visits with the elderly**—When church members are homebound or living alone, it can be great fun to have several guests stop by for an evening of conversation.

FINAL THOUGHTS ABOUT...SINCERITY

Delivering fruit baskets doesn't guarantee community—but delivering fruit baskets can *lead* to community. There's something real and tangible about being given a gift—especially one as memorable as the gift of healthy, fresh fruit.

As you implement this program in your church, remind the people making deliveries to linger, to ask questions, to welcome recipients into a deeper relationship with them, with your church, and with God.

"FORSAKE NOT AN OLD FRIEND."
—APOCRYPHA